LIFE BEGINS AT
INCORPORATION

Cartoons and Essays by Matt Bors

Life Begins at Incorporation / Matt Bors
Includes cartoons

The cartoons in this book were published in various outlets over the years.
Some of the writing appeared in different forms on the author's website,
Cartoon Movement, and in *The Oregonian*.

ISBN: 978-0-9889271-0-0

First Edition (April 2013)

Printed in Canada

www.mattbors.com

CONTENTS

David Anton Falk Poems
Polylounge

FOREWORD

BY JACK OHMAN

 Some people say that editorial cartooning is dying. In many—but not all—quarters in journalism, it is dying, but not from old age, or disease. More specifically, it is dying because of two reasons.

It's being murdered and it's committing suicide.

Simultaneously.

I won't name names, and the reasons are many, but I think one of the main reasons is that a lot of cartoonists have lost sight of their mission. Sometimes, they won't even make a case for their own survival. But I can tell you what their mission should be, and it can be summed up in two words:

Kick ass.

Hard.

Okay, that's three. But I can sum up kick-ass cartooning in one word.

Bors.

Okay, that's a name. But I can tell you, in fact, that cartooning is alive and well under the point of Matt Bors' pen and the tip of his brush.

When I first met Matt a few years ago, he was a 25-year-old artist who had just moved to Portland from Canton, Ohio, where I suspect the hardness of the climate and the bleakness of the economy had a lot to do with shaping his worldview. Matt was one of the many young people who had migrated to Portland, which I liken to Paris in the 1920s or New York in the 1950s for young, creative people.

I was the cartoonist for *The Oregonian*, and, while creative, not on the lower end of the demographic. In getting to know Matt, I found an artist who truly grasped the essential function of a hard-hitting editorial cartoonist: be a great writer, be a great analyst, be a great illustrator, and be a great journalist. It's hard to find a cartoonist who has all of those qualities rolled up into one package. Matt does.

In his cartoon journalism, Matt traveled to Afghanistan to see first-hand what was happening on the ground. He went to Haiti to observe the aftermath of the devastating earthquake. He edited and spoke to the world's cartoonists in his role at the Cartoon Movement. He read about and observed the foibles of the various elected officials in the United States. In so doing, Matt found out something it took me rather a long time to discover: cartooning is actually a writing job. A friend of mine once observed that editorial cartoons were columns in haiku form, but his cartoons are, more accurately, a kind of illustrated poetry; there are just enough words to convey narrative with pictures, but not discursive or overly verbose.

There are two schools in American editorial cartooning today: the establishment humorists and the alternative ironists. I put Matt in the latter category, because he never, ever just makes a joke. Ever. The temptation to simply amuse is overwhelming, and, God knows, we can all use a laugh, but his work conjures up more of a primordial snort, or a rueful groan. Or, a quiet "Whoa." You will never see a cartoon of his that has the president sitting at his desk talking into a phone, a couple sitting on a sofa watching television making an observation, a TV reporter standing in front of a federal building saying something, a car labeled "The Economy" driving off a cliff, or one of the many devices that may have contributed to the weakening of this beautiful artform. Now, having said that, Matt would also probably cringe at my saying that he sometimes makes me laugh, period. I won't tell anyone.

Matt's work is original because he is original. He didn't re-invent cartooning, and neither did I, and neither did a lot of other cartoonists, but he figured out a way to move the ball down the field (cartoon metaphor alert) in a way that is refreshing and idiosyncratic. Being original is enough, frankly. He figured out a way to channel his own voice into his work, which is really all you can ask of an artist in this society. I can think of a lot of talented people in this profession that I love, but Matt really does rise to the top, because he harnesses his own experience and emotions.

A Bors cartoon is uncompromising, in the way that young men in their twenties can be uncompromising. Why should they compromise? The world is theirs to take over and run; the compromisers are sometimes rewarded, but usually it's the pathfinders who win. And Matt has won already: he's won the Herblock Prize, the Society of Professional Journalists' Sigma Delta Chi Award, and, along with me, was a finalist for the Pulitzer Prize in 2012, which was won by the similarly uncompromising former Portlander Matt Wuerker. Now, I can tell you something that is absolutely true: I could not have been happier with that outcome and neither could he that day (sniffle, wipe nose on sleeve, being all big about it), which we spent together, hanging out in Portland. In fact, of the three finalists, all three were from Portland and two were named Matt.

Don't tell me the system isn't rigged.

As you go through this book, which was funded by Matt's fans (me included) with Kickstarter, you will see what you already know: his work kicks the aforementioned ass. His politics are self-evident, but he doesn't protect anyone, which is as it should be.

I talk to Matt quite frequently, usually every few days. Almost invariably, Matt is drawing. These calls can take place at nine in the morning or nine in the evening, but I can tell you that a truly motivated, passionate artist—he has a pen nib *tattooed on his arm*—really doesn't stop creating. They *have* to. Why?

They have something to say.

In a perfect environment, the reader forms a bond with that artist. On some level, in a strange but bizarrely beautiful way, the reader comes to feel they somehow know the artist.

Matt Bors is someone worth knowing, and his work, his voice, his mind, and his heart speak to all of us. Keep listening, and you will hear a beautiful sound:

The sound of an ass being kicked.

Jack Ohman is the editorial cartoonist for The Sacramento Bee, *where his work appears in 200 newspapers through Tribune Media Services. He has won most major cartooning awards, as well as the Nobel Prize in Physics and a Daytime Emmy for Best Supporting Actress. He's old enough to be Matt's dad—barely.*

LIFE BEGINS AT INCORPORATION

PREFACE

THE WORLD IS RUN BY ASSHOLES

The men in charge of ancient Pompeii did a fairly good job of destroying the city before a giant cloud of ash swiftly finished the job for them. The city was run by corrupt liars. Most of the population knew this, but were powerless to incite change. How do we know? Because preserved on Pompeii's walls is political graffiti ruthlessly mocking those in power.

Political cartoonists are some of the only people keeping score in society, and I hope a few of my cartoons will be unearthed from the ruins of our forthcoming apocalypse as proof that we weren't all on board with the way things were going.

The cartoons in this book cover a period of American decline I don't think has been fully accounted for yet. We're halfway through a "lost decade" we worried about when our financial system crashed in 2008. According to indicators used by most economists—the growth of Wall Street, the Dow, employment rates—we're bouncing back from the recession. But for people who have lost homes, delayed retirement, been locked out of careers, accepted new ones for lower pay, and become mired in a lifetime of student debt, the economy doesn't quite seem on the upswing.

Americans have lost faith in nearly every institution, beginning with their government. Approval of Congress sits around nine percent, lower than used car salesmen, lice, and Nickleback. Nearly everyone else in a position of power has proven to be just as detestable. The priests are molesters, the homophobes are gay, the athletes are juicers, the memoirists are frauds, your friends from high school post militantly dumb and easily disprovable things on Facebook on a daily basis.

Many of my cartoons are motivated by the urge to call bullshit. Looking back on them now, I'd happily put my record on the issues as a lowly political cartoonist up against any highly compensated pundit in Washington. The pundits share something in common with those in power: the total absence of a sense of humor. Which makes bringing them down a notch that much more satisfying.

If you should think I'm a relentlessly negative curmudgeon, I will shake my fist at you and say that I'm not. There are innumerable things in today's world that I find unobjectionable or even inspiring marks of genuine human progress. But none of them compel me to draw cartoons. My work serves to humor the afflicted and afflict the humorless.

Not that it changes our circumstances. The world is run by assholes. It's been this way for some time now. Sometimes the only thing you can do is mark up public surfaces and get everyone to laugh at the people running things. It's a small form of resistance, a minor annoyance at best to those in power. But if they insist on doing us this way, I'm at least going to make them come out every morning and repaint the damn walls.

Matt Bors
Portland, Oregon
March 2013

LIFE BEGINS AT INCORPORATION

"The night belongs to Dr Pepper. And the next year too." – Dr. Pepper (via Twitter)

 Jonathan Frieman had been driving down Highway 101's carpool lane for years hoping to get pulled over. When he finally was, in 2012, he was ticketed $478 for driving solo. He maintained he had every right in the world to be in the carpool lane since there was another person with him: articles of incorporation for his company, the JoMiJo Foundation. Marin County's Traffic Court did not agree. If they had found that his corporation was a person, however, another ticket would have been in order. He forgot to buckle up JoMiJo.

Corporations are people on paper, and they have a lot more say over things than those of us who are old-fashioned people with our lousy "bodies." In 2010, the Supreme Court's decision in the *Citizens United* case essentially ruled that money is speech, knocking down limits on corporate spending in elections. I'm guessing you don't have as much money as an oil company, but that's okay—the oil company worked its way up from humble origins and has a lot to say about politics.

"Corporations are people, my friend," Mitt Romney famously told a man at the Iowa State Fair in 2011. "Everything corporations earn ultimately goes to people. Where do you think it goes?" ("The Cayman Islands" would have been a good response.) Romney was quickly savaged for his tone-deaf devotion to corporate personhood, but his opinions didn't differ in any substantial way from anyone else in national politics. Democrats who loudly proclaimed the *Citizens United* decisions to be the End of Fairness didn't seem to have a problem accepting help from the new shady groups it allowed to form.

Having a business be a legal entity makes perfect sense. That legal presence gives the company a standing that can be challenged in court. You can't file a lawsuit against, say, a piece of pie for not being delicious enough. (Not that I've ever had this problem.) But if a pie company's delicious goods cause cancer, perhaps you should have recourse. Where the problem comes in is giving corporations constitutional rights, an idea conceived of long ago that has reached full maturity in recent decades.

In 1816, the Supreme Court determined that corporations had rights that couldn't be taken away by the state. But it wasn't until the Fourteenth Amendment was passed that the corporate civil rights movement hit the big time. That amendment, you'll recall, was passed after the Civil War and famously ensured that people of all races have citizenship and equal protection under the law. The Supreme Court didn't get around to deciding black people could marry white people for almost another hundred years, but in 1886 they eagerly established corporations as protected "persons" in *Santa Clara County v. Southern Pacific Railroad*. This was further ensconced into law two years later in *Silver Mining Co. v. Pennsylvania*, and with that, the American Free Enterprise System was off to a great start!

Since then, there have been a steady stream of cases upholding and building on these decisions, not to mention laws and tax codes that make life as a corporation pretty breezy. Corporations have argued before courts—successfully—that they have rights to free speech, a Fourth Amendment right to privacy, and are protected from discrimination by, I guess, people who are racist against corporations.

In 1933, J.C. Penney successfully won a case against Florida communities trying to keep out chain stores on grounds that they faced discrimination. In 2009, J.C. Penney paid out $50,000 to a black woman in a racial discrimination lawsuit after their salon told her: "We don't do African American hair." I guess she knows how that poor company must have felt back in the day.

Today, corporation-Americans can do more than flesh-Americans in some respects. A corporation-American can jump on a plane and establish itself in another country far easier than you can. They can cross international borders with ease, dump unlimited amounts of cash into political campaigns, and even pollute water and air. You yourself can't go around belching tons of toxic waste into the atmosphere; your neighbors would complain. But your company can—for a profit!

Corporations get to do all the cool stuff without the legal and corporeal downsides that having a body entails. Deplorable businesses will never be strapped to a gurney and executed by the state like many people who can't afford a good lawyer. The worst that could happen to a corporation-American is the government could revoke their charter.

It didn't even seem this bad in a not-so-long-ago time called the nineties. Remember when sports arenas were all named after local oligarchs and industry barons? At some point they figured out they could relinquish a sliver of narcissism and make even more money by releasing the naming rights to corporations. Now we have exciting names like Verizon Arena, Pepsi Center, and JeldWen Field.

In early 2013, Florida Atlantic University sold the naming rights to their sports stadium for $6 million. It will now have the eloquent name of GEO Group Stadium, after GEO Group Inc., the second-largest private prison company in America. Imprisoning people—what an admirable business strategy for a school to applaud!

There is something beautiful about that to me. Some days, it feels like we have reached the pinnacle of capitalism. But I shouldn't rush to judgment. I'm sure new offensive heights can be attained.

As the idea of what a corporation is and should be continues to expand, I wouldn't be surprised if one gets elected president someday. I just hope it's a decent one, like Bounty paper towels, instead of an evil dick like Marlboro. I bet Bounty would make an okay president.

We do sort of treat corporations as people-like now, which is a little creepy. We love them, are loyal to them, and if they break our trust we take our business to one who understands our needs better. They're like friends and lovers, except they are electronics companies and brands of flavor-dusted potato chips.

When the Cinemark company reopened its theatre in Aurora, Colorado, after the 2012 mass shooting, it invited the relatives of slain victims and promised them free tickets. Everyone fumed: pretty rude behavior from Cinemark. Apologize now.

But doesn't the premise that Cinemark can express any proper sentiments about murder accept that the company is anything more than a legal construct that funnels money to shareholders via movie ticket sales? Cinemark can say "We are now showing *Django Unchained*" and "We are open from 9:30 a.m. to 11:20 p.m. on Wednesday," but can Mr. Cinemark truly convey any worthwhile feelings on human beings gunned down inside...it? Should we expect it to?

The 2003 documentary *The Corporation* takes the premise that if corporations are people, then they are diagnosable psychopaths, incapable of feeling guilt, lying with ease, and lacking consideration for the safety

of others. When you think about it, they do come off a bit like self-centered assholes without empathy. Sure, sociopaths have a place in society. But it doesn't seem like a good idea to make that place the tippy top.

America's founders did see early signs of this crap.

The conception moment of the American Revolution is typically told as an anti-tax tale. The colonists, upset with the Tea Act, threw a fit and tossed some tea into the Boston Harbor. No taxation without representation! But there's an anti-big-business angle to the story.

Ahem! History books open. The British Crown granted the East India Company a monopoly over tea imports, establishing their right to tax the colonies. Colonists would have to buy this specific tea from this specific company and pay the tax. Funny enough, many members of the British government owned stock in the company, so making the decision to grant it a monopoly was an easy one. This ploy was going to ruin the local economy (the much-loved "small businesses" of future America) and people went appropriately apeshit.

Imagine being forced to buy only Starbucks coffee. There'd be a revolution before the workday even got underway.

BORS

One of the key motivators in the birth of our nation was essentially a rebellion against unfair collusion between a giant company and a corrupt government. Maybe one day we'll get as fed up as the colonists did. Over 200 fiscal years later, the interests of businesses—now deemed people—have our democracy in its death throws. Ah, the circle of life.

DESTINATION: AFGHANISTAN

"Rule number one in politics is: never invade Afghanistan."
– Harold Macmillan, former British Prime Minister

 In August of 2010, at the age of 26, I embarked on my first trip outside of the United States. To Afghanistan. My colleague Ted Rall had been there a number of times before, including to Northern Afghanistan as the bombs fell in late 2001. He was working on a new book and was planning to travel independently through the war-torn country during the hottest month of the year. Did I want to tag along?

"Most everyone who goes comes back," he assured me. "The odds are really in your favor." We were approaching the tenth year of American war in the country and the violence was as high as it had been since the initial invasion. We would stick to cities in the north and west, he said, avoiding the heavy fighting in the southeast along the border with Pakistan. Another cartoonist, Steven Cloud, would join us.

"Of course," I said, because I am a person who says yes to bad ideas. After spending the better part of a decade behind a drawing table making cartoons about our nation's various foreign adventures, I wanted to take one of my own, sans killing anyone. America has had "boots on the ground" in Afghanistan my entire adult life. The least I could do was actually see the place my (meager) tax dollars have been paying to destroy and rebuild. Afghans live their entire lives there. I figured I could make it a month. I brought a lot of sketchbooks.

America's plan in Afghanistan has always been deeply flawed. Setting one trillion dollars on fire after 9/11 would have been a better idea than the one we went with. That brief monetary inferno

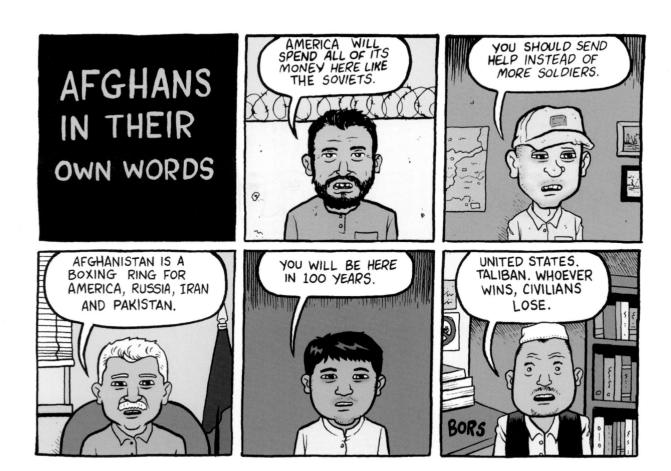

could have at least provided something for homeless people to warm their hands over. It most likely wouldn't have resulted in tens of thousands of dead people.

If you think about it, the most devastating and lasting effect of the World Trade Center towers falling was something the hijackers did not anticipate. Had the towers not fallen, it's easy to imagine foreign policy in the first decade of the 21st century proceeding rather mildly. Instead, someone had to pay for the attack, so we invaded one of the poorest nations on earth to "take the fight to the terror-ists" before diverting all of our resources to Iraq. Then we got our eye back on the ball with Obama's troop surge, which got us out of war by sending more people to fight in one. Anyway, we've been in Afghanistan a while now. People young enough to have only dim memories of 9/11 are now eligible to fight and die in the war it created.

Those young soldiers will be in good company. The 9/11 hijackers may have trained in Afghani-stan, but they weren't from there. A lot of Afghans don't know what the hell we are talking about when we talk about the World Trade Center. A 2011 survey by the International Council on Security and Development of 15- to 30-year-old men living in rural southern Afghanistan—the most violent region of the country—revealed 92 percent had no clue what "this event that the foreigners call 9/11" even is.

MUHAMMAD SHAH

HAMID KARZAI?
"HE'S GOOD."

BARACK OBAMA?
"HE'S GOOD."

GEORGE BUSH?
"KILL HIM."

SAYID ATAH MUHAMMAD

"YOU ARE AMERICANS?"

YES.

"WHICH PROVINCE
ARE YOU FROM?"

MY FRIENDS ARE
FROM NEW YORK.
I AM FROM OREGON.

"WHERE IS OREGON
PROVINCE?"

NORTH OF
CALIFORNIA
PROVINCE.

"ARNOLD SHWINZIGGER!"

"Never heard of it," 16-year-old Abdul Ghattar told the *Wall Street Journal*. "I have no idea why the Americans are in my country."

While their lack of awareness about 9/11 offends our sense of self-importance, I don't think for a minute that most Americans could identify the two languages spoken by most Afghans. (The people are "Afghans," by the way. "Afghanis" is their currency.)

My trip was uncomfortable, disturbing, dirty, and wonderful. The Afghan people were eager to talk and laugh and host. On the surface, they smiled; underneath, life balanced on a knife's edge. Many people I met gracefully endure living conditions that would send most first-worlders into a puddle of self-pity. I spoke to shopkeepers, students, contractors, police, and a member of the terrorist organization Hezb-e-Islami. (He stayed across the hall from us in a dingy hotel with a bullet hole in the window and invited us over for a chat. Topics covered: killing Russians, the Quran, sex.) No women, though. They still wore bright blue full-body burqas in most areas outside Kabul, and I saw more women's faces on the billboards encouraging them show up to vote than I saw in real life.

We had arrived in the country during campaign season. Election posters already faded by the hot sun blanketed every storefront and barbed wire–topped wall, announcing each of the 2,500 candidates vying for 249 seats. Political parties themselves were outlawed at the time, so after only a few years of democracy they were having more genuinely competitive elections than ours. Most Afghans are illiterate, so candidates were identified by randomly assigned icons, like two laptops, one pistachio, or three rickshaws. In a famously landlocked country, one candidate was represented by a sailboat. I wondered how many people had ever seen one.

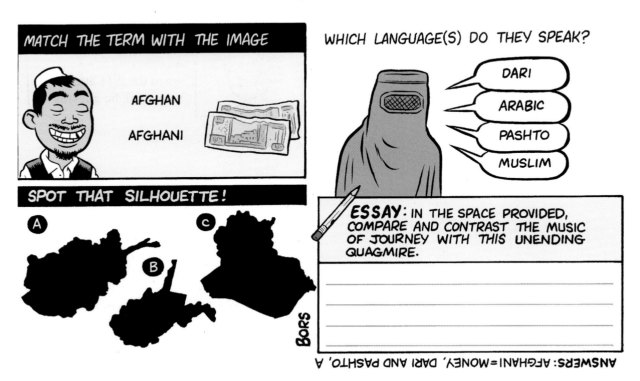

I traveled the country at a time when Americans were struggling to understand Obama's religion, some people were trying to block a mosque from being in lower Manhattan, and a Christian lunatic in Florida announced his plan to publicly set some Qurans on fire. Word of all three made it over to Afghanistan. The abstraction of a Quran-burning in Florida quickly solidifies when it directly increases risks on your life.

"Now I see on TV how Americans don't want Muslims to pray near the site of the trade towers," a young man named Aziz told me. He had fled to Pakistan during the Taliban's reign and had returned a few years ago—I often met people with harrowing life stories like that. Now he was doing work for a Russian cell phone subcontractor in Herat. "They still think we are all terrorists."

"I used to believe America stood for Democracy and freedom of religion," he said. "I don't believe in America anymore."

Afghanistan has been torn apart by decades of constant war. First, by invading Soviet forces, then over a decade of bloody civil war between the Taliban and various other factions. In many ways life has improved for Afghans since our invasion. Paved roads connect major cities, electricity is more widely available, and cell phone coverage exists in 11,000-foot mountain passes and mud-hut villages

Study: Kids Who Can't Remember Start Of Afghanistan War Now Old Enough To Die In It

"It's about the dead guy, Osama, right?"
- Ryker Anderson, 19

Travis, 18, who is stationed in Kabul, was playing trucks when the 9/11 attacks happened, he guesses.

alike. People are no longer being executed in sports stadiums. These are definitely positive changes you can point to. But security is practically nonexistent. Paved roads are nice if you get to use them, even nicer if they're safe to drive on (which they're not). Almost a decade after the Taliban was ousted, only to return with a growing insurgency, the endless conflict seemed to be wearing on everyone.

You don't have the same sort of certainty about tomorrow or faith in government that Americans have after you've seen multiple regimes fall during your lifetime. Money is treated like something that could be worthless tomorrow morning. When we paid a manager of a hotel for our stay, he asked for a different $100 bill when he noticed a small tear in the one we gave him. Crisp, new U.S. bills are accepted by moneychangers; old crumpled bills can take a hike. Argue all you like about the bill's true value, but if everyone disagrees with you, you're the one who's wrong. What would he do with this slightly torn piece of paper with Ben Franklin's head on it? He'd love if it was worth the same, but it was out of his control.

There's a common saying in the Muslim world: *Inshallah*, meaning "god willing" or "if god wills it." It is said as a wish or a goodwill blessing. In Afghanistan it's often used as dark humor. We asked our first driver, Javid, if he thought there would be a Taliban biker gang on the road from Taloqan to Mazar-i-Sharif. (This was an actual thing going on at the time.)

"*Inshallah*," he smiled. In other words, we'd all find out together.

Most Afghans I talked with seemed resigned to the rampant criminality and fraud that has defined the new government. While rejecting the Taliban, many people I met expressed antipathy toward the spectacularly corrupt government, which keeps Hamid Karzai in power a decade after the United States installed him as president.

In Aziz's view, democracy wasn't working out very well. "Karzai controls everything," he said. Bribes and nepotism were the real levers of power. "Is this what American democracy is supposed to be?" he asked. I told him that it was.

The Hezb-e-Islami guy in the dingy hotel preferred the old system. "We need Sharia. That is all," he said, simply. Some people please easy.

But the warlords and business class prefer this government, where money is king and manipulating votes is never hard. Fake voter registration cards are printed by the thousands in Pakistan. After voting, people told me, you can scrub the purple ink off your finger with bleach and head to another polling place. Or even easier: bribe everyone who works there.

In the last days of August, while I was in the western city of Herat, campaign workers and candidates started being gunned down in the streets. Seemed like a good time to leave.

AN ENTIRE GENERATION OF AMERICANS IS GROWING UP HAVING NEVER KNOWN LIFE IN PEACETIME.

FOR THEM, FIGHTING IN THE SAME FOREIGN ADVENTURE AS THEIR PARENTS WILL SEEM COMMONPLACE.

LIKE GETTING A JOB AT THE SAME FACTORY IN THE OLDEN DAYS, SON!

OCCUPYING IRAQ AND AFGHANISTAN WON'T BE SEEN AS OUTRAGEOUS QUAGMIRES, SIMPLY THE WAY THINGS ARE.

WE MIGHT AS WELL PROTEST THE SKY BEING BLUE.

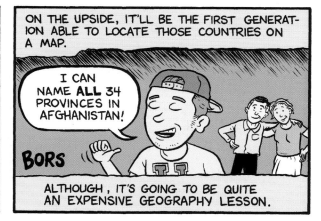

ON THE UPSIDE, IT'LL BE THE FIRST GENERATION ABLE TO LOCATE THOSE COUNTRIES ON A MAP.

I CAN NAME **ALL** 34 PROVINCES IN AFGHANISTAN!

BORS

ALTHOUGH, IT'S GOING TO BE QUITE AN EXPENSIVE GEOGRAPHY LESSON.

It's hard to tell what Afghans expect to grow more in their country: violence or corruption. A policy analyst I met in a Kabul restaurant guarded by blast walls said the NGO community has learned to mark progress at a snail's pace. On election day, 14 people were gunned down. Election oversight workers invalidated 1.3 million ballots out of the 5.6 million cast. The policy analyst expected as much. "This isn't Sweden," he said. "At least they're taking control of their own corrupt elections."

AFGHANISTAN MAY BE A THIRD WORLD WARZONE, BUT THEY ARE SURPASSING AMERICA IN A LOT OF WAYS.

THEIR CONSTRUCTION EFFORTS MAKE US LOOK DOWNRIGHT LAZY.

EVEN DILAPIDATED SHACKS ARE OUTFITTED WITH ENVIRONMENTALLY FRIENDLY LIGHTBULBS...

AND AFGHANS WALK AROUND TEXTING ALL DAY ON CHEAP CELL PHONES.

PHONE CARDS!

THEIR DRIVERS TALK ON THEIR PHONES MORE THAN AMERICANS DO...

AH, IT IS MY **SECOND** WIFE NOW WHO CALL!

SITAAR RING TONE.

EVEN ON A 12,000 FT. MOUNTAIN PASS WITH NO GUARDRAIL.

CAN YOU CALL THEM BACK LATER?!

WE STILL HAVE THEM BEAT ON ROAD SAFETY.

BORS

AT A DINGY HOTEL IN CHAGHCHARAN, A MEMBER OF THE TERRORIST ORGANIZTION HEZB-E-ISLAMI STAYED ACROSS THE HALL FROM US.

HE INVITED US OVER FOR A CHAT.

HE SPOKE FONDLY OF HIS TIME KILLING SOVIETS AND THE NEED FOR SHARIA LAW.

ALLAH MADE THESE WAYS TO LIVE. IT'S ALL VERY LOGICAL.

ALLAH IS THE CAUSE OF EVERY-THING.

MY FRIEND CLOUD CHIMED IN.

SO WHAT CAUSED ALLAH?

OH, SNAP!

EXCUSE ME. ALLAH NEEDS NO CAUSE.

BORS

HE HAD KILLED BEFORE. WE DIDN'T PUSH IT.

MAKES SENSE.

VERY LOGICAL.

IN THE SMALL TOWN OF TALOQAN WE STAY AT THE ARIANA HOTEL AND WEDDING HALL, THE ONLY PLACE IN TOWN WHERE FOREIGNERS CAN SLEEP.

I HEAD DOWN TO THE LOBBY TO CHECK US IN...

SO YOU ARE AMERICANS?

YES.

AMERICA IS BIG BOSS COUNTRY. WANTS TO BE *BIG BOSS* OF *ENTIRE PLANET!*

UH... NOT ALL AMERICANS ARE LIKE THAT.

WE DON'T WANT TO BE THE BIG BOSS!

BORS

RELAX, AMERICAN. I AM, HOW YOU SAY, MESSING WITH YOU!

22

MORE LIKE OBUMMER

"We are the ones we've been waiting for." – Barack Obama

 When Barack Obama delivered his second inaugural address, the commentariat agreed: this guy was now full-on liberal. In his speech, Obama mentioned social inequality, the existence of gays, and the concept that climate change is a thing that is happening.

Writing in the *New Yorker*, the mighty liberal tone-setter, editor David Remnick, declared this version of the president to be "Barack Obama without apology—a liberal emboldened by political victory and a desire to enter the history books with a progressive agenda."

Was this the end of the four-year rope-a-dope strategy we'd been hearing about? No more of the dreary, bipartisan fetishist who emerged the moment he finished his last rousing campaign speech in 2008, but an actual fighter?

Well, I don't think it's too early to say that no, Obama's second term will not usher us into a new era of liberal awesomeness.

Obama rode a wave of Bush resentment into office to become our first black president and the mood of the nation changed overnight. We—those who were frazzled from a decade of war, lies, and secrecy—weren't just done with the Bush Era, we had a new leader who actually seemed promising, if only by virtue that his short Senate career hadn't provided him enough time to let us down.

Obama would bring our troops home, restore the rule of law, expel lobbyists from Washington, be transparent, make us breakfast in bed. When he assembled a cabinet completely devoid of liberals,

instead filled with conservative Democrats, Wall Street insiders, and a few holdovers scraped from the rotting carcass of the Bush administration, I suppose it was an effort in more transparent government. Because everyone should have seen what was coming next.

If you were able to look past the speeches and the incredible "oh shit!" moment of joy that came with seeing our first black president (not to mention a man who seemed familiar with pop culture of the last, oh, forty years), you could see Obama's actual positions weren't all that liberal in the first place. Hell, he never even said they were. We made that up.

Swiftly in Obama's first term, promises were abandoned, plans reversed, ambitions scaled back. This was Washington, not the welcoming land of Care Bears. Nice words here are only worth the amount of money your K Street lobbyist has bundled with them. Why did Obama seem so devoted to conceding ground to cravenly hostile Republicans? His negotiation tactics gave a mile and asked for an inch back. He was a typical Democrat, after all.

But midway through his first term, Obama's preternatural calm was beginning to approach aloofness. We avoided another Great Depression, the saying goes, but most Americans were still living in crisis. Healthcare is where he made a play for a fight.

When healthcare reform finally took center stage in 2009, Democrats presented a problematic private-based reform bill based on the Republicans' own plan from 1994. Suddenly, the Right thought it unconstitutional—and death panels, oh my! Liberals ignored the reform's origins at the conservative Heritage Foundation think tank. Democrats quickly shuffled the promised true reform—a public option—out the door.

The center of debate in American politics had swung far to the right. Democrats were acting like Republicans. Republicans were acting like they needed prescription medication. You were either with Obamacare or against it.

Team sports worry me, which is why I like political cartooning. It's a solo, sort-of negative profession. No parties. A lot of people expect you to pull punches and focus only on the latest weekly rantings of the Right. And, oh, they make it so very easy. But this game isn't like that. There are enough people promoting all the good work our leaders are doing. I can't make those laudatory cartoons while Democrats resemble the conservatives in most Western democracies.

Of course, there is no good time to bring any of this up. There are always worse evils banging on the door for defenders to point to. Do you want John McCain to be president? Mitt Romney? How about Hitler?!

Had John McCain taken office as president on January 21, 2008, however, he most likely also wouldn't have delivered on many of his campaign promises. McCain's pledge to end torture and close Guantanamo would have been abandoned in the face of Republican opposition, and the idea of a troop surge in Afghanistan and ultimately leaving that country would have dragged on longer than he had told us. He would have deported illegal immigrants in record numbers. He might even have killed a U.S. citizen, not to mention plenty of bystanders, in various drone strikes around the world.

Had that been the case, I would count on liberals to lament the country's slide into fascism under "The McCain Regime." As it is now, they quietly register light annoyance with Obama's handling of these issues before moving straight into how damn insane the Republicans are. (Answer: very insane.)

Supporters of the president just trust the man. "Look at the good he's done," they say. Indeed, Obama hasn't all been bad. Obama is the first president to tepidly support gay marriage on a states' rights level. But for that kind of half-measure, he gets no cookie. You're supposed to think gays are equal. "And by the way," they say, "isn't he a genuinely nice guy who means well?"

WE ALL KNOW THE SCENE: A WHITE GUY AND A BLACK GUY APPROACH EACH OTHER ON A DARK STREET.

TENSIONS MOUNT AS THEY CLOSE IN.

WILL THE STRANGER ATTACK?

YES!

HEY! EXCITED ABOUT OBAMA?

DID YOU CRY? I CRIED.

NICE HOODIE!

BORS

THANKFULLY, THE NICE MAN ESCAPES AND WARNS HIS FAMILY.

STEER CLEAR OF THOSE PEOPLE FOR A FEW WEEKS.

IT'S LIKE THEY'RE ALL HIGH OR SOMETHING.

In the jubilation around Obama's win, there was a moment where it seemed we could heal the racial divide in America. It lasted a good ten, fifteen minutes.

Obama is a kind of Rorschach blot president. One person sees a Good and Decent Family Man, another sees a Socialist Usurper with a Broccoli-Nazi for a wife. I see a guy who is probably the best our current system can produce—which doesn't bode well for the system.

Obama became president during a time when fundamental change was required. He needed to make the case for government's helpful role in society the way Ronald Reagan made his presidency an argument against it. There may not be a right-wing president to take issue with for quite a while. The Dems are it. The GOP has positioned itself to be a permanent minority party. Most of the destructive economic policies and Bush-era war powers remain intact and Obama hasn't surprised us with any bold progressive era yet.

I know. You can only do so much. But you have to do enough.

"Wake up and smell the coffee BOY. I am going TEABAG at your tea party if you can figure that one out you RACIST SOB" – William

LIFE BEGINS AT INCORPORATION

BIPARTISAN COMPROMISE

LIFE BEGINS AT INCORPORATION

LIFE BEGINS AT INCORPORATION

I hope you are not suffering from this debilitating illness. There is always an uptick in cases during election years. Symptoms include loudly declaring that Republicans are even worse, ignoring problems with Democrats, and randomly reminding people that Ralph Nader ruined the 2000 election.

HOMOPHOBIA IS GAY

"We don't have to debate about what we should think about homosexual activity. It's written in the Bible." – Ted Haggard

"If I were 21 in this society, I would identify myself as a bisexual." – Ted Haggard

 When I was a teenager in Ohio, one way I passed the time was arguing with strangers about religion. Once while skateboarding in a church parking lot, I got into a debate with a kid my age who was newly into Jesus. He was super excited to tell me about the Lord. He was also registering a steady ping on my gaydar. We batted back and forth with the standard atheist and Christian arguments; I mentioned evolution, he mentioned that people would "just go around killing everyone" if there wasn't a god.

"How do you know your religion is any more true than other religions?" I asked him.

"I know the power of Jesus Christ," he said. "If it wasn't for him I'd be gay right now."

I didn't have the heart to break it to him, but my brain was shouting, "Dude, you *are* gay right now!" Time would fix this boy's head, I figured—the "power of Jesus" can only substitute sex for so long.

He could have grown up to be the prayer outreach coordinator for the National Organization for Marriage, could be working right now to preserve "traditional marriage."* But chances are this rather attractive man went to college a few months later, discovered the joys of carnal knowledge, and eventually came out to his shocked and weepy parents, who at some point got the hell over it because they love their son.

The kid's in luck. Public opinion on gay rights in America has only moved steadily in one direction—approval.

Now, the number of people who have gone from believing that their gay friends and neighbors deserve equal rights to believing that gayness is an evil sin that must be eradicated is probably zero. If you find me someone who did make that backwards shift, I will bet you my entire bank account that this someone is having trouble accepting their sexuality. Being anti-gay is about the gayest thing you can be.

My colleague Ruben Bolling laid this out perfectly in a 2007 Tom the Dancing Bug cartoon, "New Gay Stereotype."

"Look, homosexuality is a sin," says a balding conservative to his partner. "It says so right in the Bible!"

"Okay," replies the man lying in bed next him. "I am so breaking up with you! You are TOO GAY!"

Around the time in the mid-2000s that gay marriage became a hot-button social issue capable of motivating millions of Americans to head to the polls to vote for gay marriage bans, a string of mighty gay-bashers fell one-by-one in a cascade of gay scandals. Colorado-based anti-gay pastor Ted Haggard admitted to smoking meth with a gay prostitute. Senator Larry Craig was caught testing out his "wide stance" in an airport bathroom. Media nationwide laughed when Reverend George Rekers said he needed to employ a young man on all his travels to "carry his luggage."

And if an unending stream of publicly outed homophobes hasn't convinced you that anyone who spends their days railing against the ills of sodomy is actually just wearing their psychology on their sleeve, we can turn to that great prover-of-things: science.

One method used in six recent studies involving a total of 784 university students found that over 20 percent of people who described themselves as "highly straight" had a subliminal personal identification with the word "gay" and images of gay couples. And—surprise!—the study also found a huge Venn diagram overlap with these internally conflicted people and those who supported anti-gay politics.

But why rely on all the subliminal stuff when you can just measure boners?

In my favorite study ever, researchers at the University of Georgia in 1996 divided self-identified straight men into two groups: those who expressed homophobic sentiments and those who didn't. The researchers attached to the men's penises a little doohicky that measures blood flow. Then the men watched short porn videos that featured straight sex, lesbian sex, and gay dude sex. All the homophobic men emphatically claimed to the researchers that they were not the slightest bit turned on by the gay dude videos. But like all men are at some point, they were betrayed by their engorged penises. The more likely the men were to be homophobic, the more likely they were to be turned on by images of gay sex.

Or, as Allen Ginsberg wrote so poetically: "A hard cock never lies."

---

* The institution of marriage they are preserving, by the way, is not of the wife-swapping, daughter-selling, incest-having, polygamist variety that has dominated much of history. The notion of romantic love, let alone female agency, didn't even enter popular consciousness until relatively recently. (One could argue we haven't fully arrived.) When feminism came along with demands like "Can we be more than secretaries?" and "Maybe pay us the same" and "Stop raping us," suddenly men had to pay more attention to the needs and desires of women if they ever hoped to land a wife, but even in such an enlightened time in America one couldn't marry someone of a different race in many states. It wasn't until *Loving v. Virginia* in 1967 that state bans on the incredible sin of marrying someone with a different skin tone were lifted by the Supreme Court, thus fully actualizing the potential and beauty of this fine institution. Then gays wanted the same and started ruining it all when Massachusetts became the first state to permit this twisted form of marriage in 2004. So the institution that is being protected by the vanguard of marriage can only be said to have really, truly, if we're being technical here, existed from June 12, 1967 to May 17, 2004. If you were married during that time: congratulations. You had a traditional marriage.

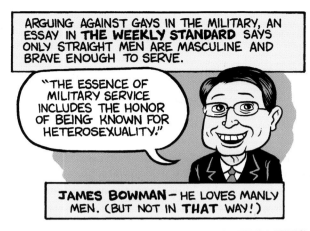

So are homophobes all gay? Yes. They're all gay. All. Gay. Until proven otherwise, at least. And the more cartoonishly full of hate they are, the more likely it is they're fighting to repress their true sexuality.

I hear you thinking, "Aha! But what about the Westboro Baptist Church? They are a whole family and can't possibly all be gay."

I have some thoughts about that.

FRED PHELPS: PROBABLY GAY

 You're right. The whole Westboro Baptist Church isn't gay. Just Fred Phelps. I'm pretty sure.

In May of 2010, I caught a Westboro picketing at Grant High School in Portland, Oregon. We're big ol' "fag-enablers" here, as the "church" likes to say. They decided to target Grant High for its apparently unacceptable number of "brute beasts who are good for absolutely nothing." A few hundred Portlanders gathered to ridicule Phelps' six followers at the picket (he was a no-show), standing alongside the protest with signs like "God Hates Fags" and "PacMan Hates Ghosts" (which—side note—I found morally problematic: PacMan *should* hate ghosts. They are attempting to murder him on a non-stop basis). One male counter-protester held a sign near a Westboro Baptist Church member that was an arrow with the text, "This guy just hit on me."

It's easy to laugh at Westboro. They're no threat at all. The group is universally despised, has zero political influence, and numbers less than 100 members. In all the hubbub around the group's crazy message of hate, we have missed what they really are: a cult.

Westboro is not simply a fringe Baptist church that really, really dislikes gay stuff. The group fits almost all the guidelines of what defines a cult: a leader, with access to an unbendable Truth that cannot be questioned; isolation from outside influences; internal cult-y jargon; constant use of unpaid labor; physical and mental abuse; an "us v. them" siege mentality; a habit of completely rejecting and denouncing those who leave; and an atrociously designed website. The cult follows a loopy interpretation of the Bible, wherein Phelps is the only person who has correctly interpreted God's word and his followers are the only ones who will survive God's judgment. It's like Noah, but instead of building an Ark to escape water, they're crafting a life raft from picket signs to escape the flood of gays. Fred Phelps chose "fags" as the focus for his cult just as other cult leaders chose obsessive focal points for theirs. Gays are to Fred Phelps what Christianity and Marxism were to Jim Jones, what UFOs are to Claude Vorilhon, and what fascism coupled with conspiracy theories are to Lyndon LaRouche.

It's unlikely Phelps pulled "fags" out of a hat. I have to imagine his obsession has something to do with a bad experience he had with a guy in a park bathroom (or, hey, a good experience he couldn't fully accept). I'm hoping someone will apply for a National Science Foundation grant to attach a doohickey to Phelps' dick and show him gay porn, just to see what happens.

Whatever the case, the people who undoubtedly pay the biggest price for Phelps' internal demons are his family. Estranged relatives say he is a physically and mentally abusive tyrant who beats them with an axe handle.

On the plus side, Phelps is unable to convince many people who aren't unlucky enough to be related to him to join the Westboro Baptist Church. And unlike, say, Charles Manson, their acts of protest provide us endless opportunity for mockery.

THINGS GOD HATES
(According To Westboro Baptist Church)

Gays	Islam
Troops	Jews
Priests	The Media
Pope Francis	America
Lady Gaga	Swedes
Obama	The World

After that Portland protest, I called up the Westboro Church, just to talk. The person who picked up the church's phone was Shirley Phelps—she's the one who runs everything while Father Fred slowly dies from the pure hate eating away at his body like a cancer. I got to know her a bit during our conversation. For example, I learned that she is under the impression God does not particularly care for homosexuality.

"This is a fag nation that is doomed. God hates fags and God hates fag-enablers," she said. The word "fag" came up a lot. I asked if everyone was going to Hell except for her church's followers. "Yup," Shirley replied. "That's the default."

I'm curious to see how the Phelps family will carry on after his death. Will the cult crumble? The third generation of Westboro members includes some kids who are now in their mid-

twenties. Given their radical ideology and isolation, it will be next-to-impossible for this generation of bigots to find suitable spouses. One of the more prominent young members, Megan Phelps-Roper, said she'd be fine remaining an unmarried virgin forever, devoting her life to the apparently fulfilling activity of constantly picketing gay people on the side of America's roads. That was before late 2011, when she fled the church with her younger sister and apologized for all the hurt she caused. Those who remain in Westboro are fighting a demented old man's losing battle. It was unthinkable a decade ago, but half of Americans now support gay marriage. "God Hates Fags" isn't quite resonating.

Before she excused herself to make more picket signs, Shirley told me, "Pushing through fag rights will be legacy of your generation." At least there's something we can agree on.

A CONSERVATIVE GROUP, ONE MILLION MOMS, HAS COME OUT AGAINST MARVEL AND DC COMICS HAVING GAY CHARACTERS.

WAIT!

RIIIP

NO. I'M **NOT** DOING THIS STRIP.

IT'S NOT **ONE MILLION** MOMS. THERE'S PROBABLY, LIKE, FORTY MOMS. **NO ONE** CARES ABOUT GAY SUPER-HEROES. **THEY'VE LOST.**

HERE.

ALL I WANT TO DRAW IS THIS.

MY POWER RING CAN CREATE ANYTHING SO LONG AS I CAN IMAGINE IT.

ANYTHING?

THERE. NOW GO ABOUT YOUR DAY.

BORS

"I think your gayness is showing, but that's ok. I know you are enlisting just as soon as you can arrange transportation to your local recruiting station. Thank you so much." – Rick

A BILL IN CALIFORNIA WOULD ALLOW THREE PEOPLE TO BE RECOGNIZED AS SOMEONE'S LEGAL PARENTS.

IF THREE IS ALLOWED, WHY NOT **FOUR MILLION PARENTS?** ALL OF WHOM ARE **ILLEGAL ALIENS!**

CAN A DOG BE MY PARENT?!

CAN I MARRY AIR?!

I DON'T KNOW WHAT IS OKAY ANYMORE I WANT MY **MOMMY!**

SINGULAR.

HETERO-NORMATIVE.

MOMMY.

BORS

THEY'RE ALL GAY

PROMINENT OUTED HOMOPHOBES

HOMOPHOBE	DATE	OOPS
Keith O'Brien	2/23/13	Cardinal in the Catholic Church forced to resign after being accused of "inappropriate contact" with subordinates during night prayers.
Ryan J. Muehlhauser	11/18/12	Michigan preacher charged with felony sex abuse of the followers he had counseled to "break away from gay life."
Zach Wyatt	5/2/12	Missouri Representative votes against an anti-bullying bill and a non-discrimination bill before he finally comes out.
Jeremy Marks	4/20/12	After coming out, this leader of an ex-gay conversion ministry had to change his group's focus a bit.
Kathryn Lehman	3/28/12	One of the writers of DOMA later repented her help for the bill when she came out as a lesbian.
Paul Babeu	2/16/12	This conservative Arizona sheriff came out after news broke that he threatened a male ex-lover with deportation.
Michael Berry	2/15/12	Conservative talk radio host who hit a parked car while leaving a gay bar. He claimed he was being framed by enemies, despite video placing him at the bar.
Greg Davis	12/16/11	This conservative Mississippi mayor ran on a "family values" platform, then came out after getting caught spending public funds at a gay sex shop.
John Smid	10/11/11	The founder of one of America's largest gay conversion ministries, Love in Action, came out in a blog post.

HOMOPHOBE	DATE	OOPS
Ian Dempsey	9/15/11	One of the many Catholic priests accused of rape.
Markku Koivisto	9/11/11	A Finnish Evangelical leader admitted to cheating on his wife with a dude.
Roberto Arango	8/29/11	This Puerto Rican GOP politico stepped down after someone found the nude photos he posted to gay dating app Grindr.
Phillip Hinkle	8/12/11	Republican lawmaker who found an 18-year-old man on Craigslist he wanted to pay for "a really good time" in his hotel room. Denies he is gay.
Albert Odulele	3/31/11	Evangelical preacher jailed for indecently assaulting a sleeping teenage boy and sexually assaulting a young preacher. WWJD?
Eddie Long	9/21/10	Virulently homophobic Baptist megachurch reverend faced a number of lawsuits from several different men alleging sexual misconduct.
Ken Mehlman	8/26/10	Former RNC Chairman who chose to resign his position rather than address rumors of his sexuality. Now in favor of same-sex marriage. Yay, I guess.
George Rekers	5/4/10	This reverend hired a twenty-year-old male prostitute from Rentboy.com for his European vacation. Claimed the man was simply there to carry his luggage. LOL.
Roy Ashburn	3/9/10	Republican Senator from California pulled over for drunk driving after leaving a gay bar in Sacramento. Now out of the closet. Careful on those roads, Roy.
Mark Buse	9/22/08	Outed while working as John McCain's chief of staff during his 2008 presidential campaign, Buse simply refused to address the matter.
Glenn Murphy, Jr.	11/9/07	Former Clark County Republican Party Chairman charged with "performing unwanted oral sex" on a man. Maybe he tripped and fell?
Richard Curtis	10/30/07	Republican Representative from Washington who filed extortion charges against a man he had sex with.
Bob Allen	7/27/07	The co-chair of John McCain's Florida campaign offered an undercover cop $20 for the chance to give him a blow job.
Larry Craig	6/11/07	Found to be soliciting sex in the bathroom of the Minneapolis Airport, Craig claimed it all was a misunderstanding deriving from his "wide stance."
Ted Haggard	11/3/07	After denying he bought meth and had sex with a male prostitute, the evagelical preacher admitted that, okay, maybe he was bi.
Mark Foley	9/28/06	A Representative from Florida, Foley resigned after sexually explicit messages to his young male congressional pages were uncovered.
James E. West	5/5/05	This mayor of Spokane, Washington, was recalled by voters after he was found posting on gay.com as "Cobra82" and accused of abusing Boy Scouts.
David Dreier	9/24/04	After losing a leadership bid in the House GOP, openly gay Congressman Barney Frank said it was due to Dreier's sexuality, a poorly-kept secret in Washington.
Ed Schrock	8/30/04	Republican anti-gay Representative from Virginia. Ended his re-election campaign after allegedly being caught on tape soliciting sex from a male prostitute.

Info compiled from gayhomophobe.com

LIFE BEGINS AT INCORPORATION

ONE NATION, UNDEREMPLOYED

"How come all we do is talk about money?" – Ri¢hie Ri¢h

The Great Recession officially ended in 2009. How's everybody doing? Did you need help uncorking the champagne?

Unless you are a one-percenter who picked up this book after mistaking the title as literal, you probably aren't ordering Cristal for the table.

Our economy has been slowly gaining ground since we bottomed out in the 2008 job-pocalypse. That oughta be good for people, right? But, turns out 121 percent of income gains made in the "recovery" went to the top one percent of the country's earners. I'm not sure how you can capture more than 100% of something. It sounds kind of greedy to me. An economist at Berkeley got to that number when figuring in the fact that incomes for most everyone else have dropped. Wages are down, household incomes are down, but don't worry, these are the job creators we're talking about. If you don't have an employment scenario figured out just yet, wait a few minutes. I'm sure some rich guy needs someone to give his shoe-shine 121 percent of their effort.

Jobs, jobs, jobs! They're everywhere. The problem with all this job-creation is the new jobs are all worse than our previous jobs, which, to be honest weren't all that rad in the first place. Some jobs, they don't even pay money, which is still a thing you need some of to live.

My mother spent the recession in multiple jobs, the most recent of which paid federal minimum wage. $7.25, baby! This is the reason why, when I hear well-paid pundits say that no one except high school kids work for minimum wage, I want fly to their home, poop on their doorstep, and set it on fire.

Stories like my mom's are the new normal. Barely scraping by and taking what you can get is the new normal. Having 500 people show up to apply for jobs at Walmart, who pursues a strategy of paying people such low wages that they qualify for government assistance, that's the new normal. Let Uncle Sam pick up the check!

If the recession taught me anything, it was how to get my dislocated shoulder back in its socket without going to the hospital. (I couldn't afford the hospital bill, so if you ever need a makeshift sling out of a flannel shirt, look no further.) But what *that* taught me was how to be scrappy and resourceful in the face of things that suck. I would have traded that life lesson for a secure career with benefits, but I'm trying to squeeze something positive out this mess.

Millennials, or Gen Y, or whatever magazines are calling the youngins these days, we're the ones getting the brunt of it in this downturn.

Maligned as a bunch of shiftless, tech-addled children raised to think they'd all get trophies, Millennials are trying to build careers out of the ruins of a job market. Amid a group that's supposed to be a bunch of entitled kids, all I see around me are young people juggling multiple jobs and unpaid

internships while trying to blot their (trigger warning!) student debt from their minds. I'd like to point out that Kim Jong-un is a Millennial running a nuclear-armed dictatorship. You give one of us a chance, we step up.

Unpaid internships are a particular flaming hoop everyone has to jump through now to land even the most mundane gig. Somewhere along the line this practice went from offering a short, genuinely helpful experience to an experiment in the outer reaches of legal exploitation.

I know people who have worked two years without pay to land a salaried gig or who float from internship to internship while bartending, waiting for something to open up in the field in which they hold a degree.

As the years drag on, the more well-off survive the wage attrition. They are the only ones who can afford working for free.

It might not be as horrendous if the young and paycheckless were graduating with degrees from a public system that leaves students with minimal tuition bills. (Hello, Canada!) As it stands now, student debt has reached a staggering one trillion dollars. One TRILLION dollars! For learning things

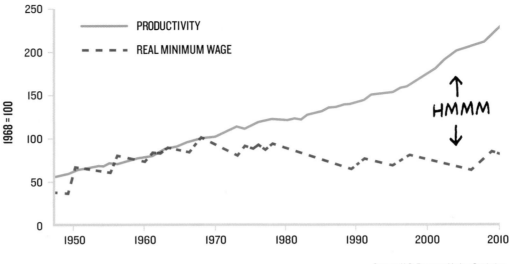

REAL VALUE OF THE MINIMUM WAGE VERSUS PRODUCTIVITY

PRODUCTIVITY

REAL MINIMUM WAGE

HMMM

Source: U.S. Bureau of Labor Statistics

in schools and there are no good jobs and oh my god I stopped to pour myself a drink since I began typing this sentence.

Let's review: we have lost a decade of economic activity. There are few stable jobs. The cost of education is so high there literally oughta be a law charging for-profit colleges with extortion. It is in this bleak landscape that people are asked to toil away their twenties in underpaid and unpaid positions that used to provide people a living.

Of course, if you're rich, there's a separate system. Arianna Huffington has made a name pursuing a debased work-for-free online media model at *The Huffington Post*. She eventually started auctioning off unpaid internships to the highest bidder—one went for $13,000. "Jumpstart your career in the blogosphere," the listing read. Hey, she's got what people want: a tiny pebble of a stepping-stone to an actual career.

That's what happens when human work is devalued to zero cents an hour and people are willing to endlessly chase the carrot. Exploiters turn their exploiting up to 11.

When I was traveling around Afghanistan writing cartoons about the people I met, an editor at *The Huffington Post* emailed me about publishing my work on their site. They said I would receive "very prominent placement" and a "link back" to my website. No pay, of course, but a link. Exposure. The currency of the web economy is attention.

I gave 'em a polite "nope."

The HuffPo business model is one that works for exactly one person. When Arianna later merged with AOL for a cool $315 million, her unpaid contributors felt duped. There's your 121 percent of economic gains right there.

SELF-OBSESSED WEB EMPRESS, ARIANNA HUFFINGTON, MERGED HER SITE WITH **AOL** FOR A WHOPPING $315 MILLION, MUCH OF IT POCKETED BY HER.

HER MEDIA EMPIRE WAS BUILT ON THE BACKS OF THE POOR SAPS SHE CONS INTO BLOGGING FOR FREE.

THE LUCKY ONES GRADUATE TO **HUFFPO HELL**, WHERE THEY'RE PAID PENNIES TO CHURN OUT TABLOID TRASH TO GENERATE TRAFFIC.

OH, AND HER LATEST BOOK IS TITLED "THIRD WORLD AMERICA."

SHE'S RICH WITH IRONY.

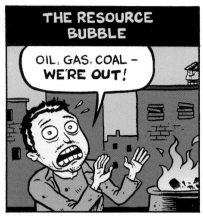

I like to dip into more journalistic comics whenever I have an excuse. In case it isn't clear, these are all real people and real quotes.

ILL COMMUNICATION

"Outside of basic intelligence, there is nothing more important
to a good political cartoonist than ill will." – Jules Feiffer

 Back when America was preparing to invade a second Muslim nation in as many years, I felt compelled to draw a cartoon about it and submit it to the student paper at the Art Institute of Pittsburgh. The comic itself wasn't very good, but I was in print for the first time. Not in a notebook, not on a scrap of butcher paper, but in an honest-to-god student newspaper run off on a copy machine, stapled together by hand, with a circulation in the high dozens. I was prime time. The editor asked me if I'd have one ready for the next issue and I thought not only would I draw it, but that maybe I'd like to draw more every week from now until I die.

At that point, I was under the impression this might have been a sane or even wise career choice.

The only other dream job I've ever had was when I was four, when I wanted to be a garbage man. I had a little garbage truck and zipped it around the basement making fake stops to pick up garbage. My dad was eager for me to grow out of this phase and aspire for a little more in life and I quickly moved on to drawing superheroes punching each other. I never thought about doing short political strips until I suddenly had something short and political to say. Looking back, I think that a garbage collector is a completely respectable career with benefits, job security, and lots of positions available. Nothing like the field I'm in now.

You are more likely to be a U.S. Senator than an editorial cartoonist. There are also far more New York Yankees than professional editorial cartoonists. And more winners of the SuperLotto. Soon, there will be more of anything and everything than political cartoonists. As far as I can tell, I appear to be the last human being in the country who took up the profession full-time.

For many decades, editorial cartooning was a cushy job where you could pull in *Mad Men* money and be the rock star of your town. Hundreds of editorial cartoonists thrived in the heyday of print media. We were attack dogs of the era before the blogosphere. Now, newsrooms' waves of layoffs and buyouts have eroded our numbers. These days, there are fewer than 60 full-time political cartoonists in the country. Print and online editors aren't hiring new ones. A once proud profession appears to be standing on its last leg. It doesn't help that some cartoonists are shooting away at that leg either.

Poorly thought-out, forced metaphors (such as the dumb sentence I wrote above) have become the main problem with the field's irrelevance. Where we once had incisive commentary, we now see harmless, overly-crosshatched gag comics. The typical editorial cartoon is a train wreck. Metaphorically it definitely is, but what I mean is that the typical editorial cartoon actually depicts a train wreck, usually accompanied by an astute label such as "Economy" or "DEBT." For the other four days of the week, replace train wrecks with hurricanes, sinking ships, flood waters, and cars heading off cliffs. Apply labels often. Repeat daily as needed.

I attribute this lazy, clichéd contingent to what I call the "Mall Caricaturist" school of editorial cartooning. You know those guys in the mall and amusement park, perhaps ill advisedly hired at a wedding you once attended, who draw whacky caricatures in that gratingly cheery, indistinguishable style of big heads and toothy grins? Those guys.

The money in newspapers and the prospect of drawing every day drew a lot of artists to the profession who then figured out how to draw in a homogenized house style and run daily news events through a metaphor machine. From that mess, out pops a cartoon. Many editors seemed to like the idea of a breezy comic not causing a stir on the editorial page and chose not to inform their artists they were supposed to have an opinion on things.

Imagine: you're given a small piece of print real estate to fill with your opinions every day. Readers are waiting for your opinions. You're paid for them. And then…you take this incredible privilege and use it to say nothing of substance. A department store ad for an underwear sale would have been a better use of the space. Buying new underwear every so often is crucial for our country's continued existence.

Pounding out formulaic cartoons like this has become a punchline itself, with a weekly parody in *The Onion* by staff cartoonist "Kelly," a curmudgeonly balding hack who inserts crying Statues of Liberty and jabs at his ex-wife into every political issue he can think of. It's brilliant, but it's a sad reminder of the moribund state of illustrated commentary.

Despite its decline, editorial cartooning does get occasional freakouts that remind you people actually care about the field.

When Barry Blitt drew Obama as a fist-bumping Muslim on the cover of the *New Yorker* in 2008 in order to satirize the right-wing caricature of him, the backlash came from the liberals it was meant to amuse. At the time, Obama supporters thought the image could be taken as literal by an ignorant public. A number of hand-wringers in Obama's corner said it would throw the election for him. If only the power of political cartoons could topple candidates, I'd be far more irresponsible with my work. Not too irresponsible, but I'd shoot for somewhere in between ending a politician's career and sparking worldwide riots.

The Danish Muhammad cartoons published in 2005 revealed you can even still cause an international incident when people see your work. Actually, without seeing it. Most of the offended Muslims who rioted over the 12 cartoons depicting the prophet Muhammad (only about half of which actually depicted him) had only heard of them through the outrage grapevine. When I wrote in defense of their existence on grounds of free speech, a woman wrote to me, nicely, calmly, "You bastard, son of a bitch, how dare you ridicule Allah's messenger? You will rot in hell, that's for sure. Your [*sic*] going to die with your face burried [*sic*] in your own shit.

"Waiting for the glorious moment of mattbors's shit-filled death!" She signed off. "May it be soon. Amen."

A joint cartoon created with Ted Rall for *The Comics Journal* depicting the near future.

So people are still paying attention to us, but a little less so with each passing year.

Boss Tweed, who ran New York with a well-liquored political machine in the 1800s, famously remarked about cartoonist Thomas Nast's critiques, "I don't care what they write about me, but stop them damn pictures!" Later Nast was credited with bringing down the corrupt Tammany Hall boss. It seems to be the single most important achievement any one of us ever accomplished. That was 136 years ago.

Nast's role in bringing down Tweed has been exaggerated over time (we tend to be a hyperbolic bunch), but the fact remains that Tweed was pissed off at the pictures in particular because he knew why they had such resonance and power: people of the day weren't as interested in articles as they were gawking at funny pictures.

Which brings us to the internet.

Today the language of the web is increasingly visual. It's memes and Facebook graphics and listicles that get around before cartoonists have a chance to get to the drawing table. What's popular now on social media isn't really that different from what was popular when Boss Tweed was Tweeding. In a sea of text, whether it's a newspaper or the web, images possess a particular power. If they didn't,

This is a response to colleagues who, every winter, draw a cartoon noting that snow is falling and therefore global warming is a myth.

Ali Farzat wouldn't have had his hands smashed in Syria for speaking out against the Assad regime. Iranian cartoonist Mahmoud Shokraiyeh wouldn't have been sentenced to 25 lashes for drawing a caricature of a member of parliament.

Cartoonists often talk about our field in romantic terms, as if drawing editorial cartoons is some grand necessity for a free and just society. It's not. If it were, we'd live in one. Democracy can continue to not function in the absence of political cartoonists. People can go through life with only LOLcats and Huffington Post slideshows to keep them grinning. But we'll be worse off for it. I want to stop regular people in their tracks and make them laugh at the things they are outraged about and scream at them for the things they aren't.

If I sound impassioned about this it's because I lack any other marketable jobs skills. I have to keep this career going until the glorious moment of my shit-filled death, or until there is an opening in my local sanitation department. May it be soon.

EDITORIAL CARTOON FOR EVERY WEEK EVER:

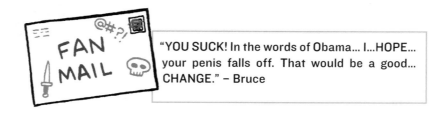

"YOU SUCK! In the words of Obama... I...HOPE... your penis falls off. That would be a good... CHANGE." – Bruce

DID YOU KNOW THAT HALLOWEEN IS A NATIONAL HOLIDAY FOR FOR EDITORIAL CARTOONISTS? IT'S TRUE! EVERY YEAR WE ISSUE THE SAME COMIC AND TAKE THE DAY OFF. **NOW IT'S YOUR TURN.** SELECT FROM THE LABELS BELOW AND PUT THEM ON THE KIDDES. USE IT TO IMPRESS YOUR LOCAL PAPER (OR MOMMY) WITH YOUR SKILLS AS A SERIOUS COMMENTATOR.

DEBT

SOCIALISM

OBAMANOMICS

LATINO VOTERS

JOB NUMBERS FOR MARCH

REVERSE RACISM

TEXTING TEENS

REALIZATION THAT YOU WILL SOMEDAY DIE

CROUCHING TEA PARTY, HIDDEN MUSLIM

"...maybe I'm not an American citizen." – Barack Obama

 An old white-haired woman in a parking lot in Ohio was going on about the president she didn't like.

"He's Muslim. He has a Muslim father," she told interviewer Chase Whitehead, a journalist compiling video of people just like this woman. Whitehead was outside of a Mitt Romney campaign event in Ohio in September of 2012, but this interview had him confused. The woman had just finished saying Obama tries to hide the fact that he attended Trinity United, Reverend Wright's Christian church in Chicago, for 20 years.

"You also think he's a Muslim?" Chase asked.

"Oh, he is a Muslim," the lady replied with a certainty you might reserve for stating your own religion. "His father was a Muslim, his father was an atheist, and his father was a Communist."

"Was his father a Muslim or was his father an atheist?"

"He's all three," she said, holding up her fingers: one-two-three.

Americans were really excited about their first black president.

The somewhat libertarian, somewhat populist, somewhat racist political movement called the Tea Party got its start three weeks after Obama was inaugurated. In 21 days on the job, Obama had not yet reversed the Great Recession that affected the entire planet's financial system. On February 29, 2009, CNBC's boisterous on-air Rick Santelli was on the floor of the Chicago Board of Trade, telling viewers how it is. The American Recovery and Reinvestment Act of 2009 had been passed two days

before and everything was not better yet. WTF? While 288 billion dollars of the stimulus package went toward the failed policy of "Tax Cuts Good," a few billion went to help people not lose their homes, which really bothered Santelli.

"This is America!" Santelli screamed. "How many of you people want to pay for your neighbor's mortgage that has an extra bathroom and can't pay their bills?!"

He had an announcement: he'd be protesting at Chicago's harbor and rallied the successful all-white male stock traders near him, which he called a "pretty good statistical cross-section of America." Within hours, video of the rant had been viewed a million times, and inspired people across the country were planning rallies as a tribute to the original 1773 Boston Tea Party, an event that if it happened today would be denounced by stock traders as violent property damage against the poor East India Company.

The somewhat libertarian, somewhat populist, somewhat racist political movement that resulted from this rant would grow, boosted by right-wing funders and Fox News, to become a political force capable of influencing the outcome of elections. This was not an unprecedented change. This was simply Republican voters calling themselves something different and wearing tri-corner hats with tea bags dangling from them. In this new era, the TEA in Tea Party stands for "Taxed Enough Already!"

They've got the taxation rhetoric on lockdown. As a sign at a rally in Chicago read, "Taxpayers are the Jews for Obama's Ovens." But the Tea Party's position on tax policies made no sense. The 2009 federal stimulus package they opposed actually lowered everyone's taxes. In fact, Americans' taxes have been decreasing for decades. If you're rich, you can snag tax rates as low as 13 percent on whatever money you don't keep in the Cayman Islands. (Just ask Mitt Romney.) Tea Partiers were older and whiter than most Americans, but their incomes reflected that of the average American: about half of them made less than $50,000 a year. In a 2010 CBS/*New York Times* poll they described the amount they paid every year in taxes as "fair." Many paid nothing. The Tea Party's rabidly anti-tax sentiment was at odds with both economic reality and the needs of many of its members. At a town hall meeting in South Carolina, a man stood up and told Rep. Robert Inglis to "keep your government hands off my Medicare."

Tea Party leaders denounced high taxes while chiding the approximately half of the country who paid no income tax—who didn't pay their "fair share." Yet broadening the tax base would mean increasing taxes for roughly half of Tea Party supporters who were "Taxed Enough Already!" Huh?

But even focusing on non-existent tax increases would have been a better platform for the party than what it quickly became. Soon, a streak of nationalism and paranoia came to define the splintered movement. That fit well within America's rich tradition of violently ignorant make-believe. Racist demagogues have nurtured our worst demons through a facade of populism all the way back to before the founding of our country. No matter the generation, some of our countrymen have always had an obsession with groups and individuals striving to undermine The American Way of Life, be they Jews, Communists, women, atheists, or SpongeBob Squarepants (he teaches homosexuality). But rarely do the nutters thrive so close to the permissible center of American politics, allowed to derail entire public policy debates with made-up notions. Almost nothing the Tea Party opposed seemed to exist: death panels, FEMA camps, gun seizure, U.N. takeovers—these are things of fantasy, not policy.

"Birthers" demanding Obama's birth certificate overran rallies toting "Go Back to Kenya" signs. Showing the black president with a bone through his nose, turns out, is bad PR. The racist loons were easy to point out (a sign at a Houston rally: "Taxpayer = Niggar [*sic*]") but the number of non-lunatic actors attending these rallies was hard to determine and subject to much debate. On the one hand, legitimate economic anxiety was ripping through every demographic at the height of the recession. Unemployment was sky high and the concept of adopting quasi-universal, market-based health care reform was new and radical to many Americans who didn't remember Republicans putting forth that exact same plan in 1994. On the other hand, you can't explain away that many people with misspelled racist signs.

Poll after poll revealed Tea Partiers as more racist, homophobic, and xenophobic than the general population. In a University of Washington poll, only 45 percent of Tea Party supporters agreed that black people were intelligent. To be fair, Tea Party opponents only buzzed in at 59 percent.

In his famous essay "The Paranoid Style in American Politics," Richard Hofstadter wrote: "In the end, the real mystery, for one who reads the primary works of paranoid scholarship, is not how the United States has been brought to its present dangerous position but how it has managed to survive at all."

You've heard about Obama's Machiavellian plan to roll out a socialist agenda. (I hope soon!) You've been told he is a foreign-born Muslim with a fake birth certificate, carrying out Kenya's long-planned coup of the United States. This is only scratching lunacy's surface.

What follows are further theories on the 44th president that people have actually put forward. Being a political cartoonist required parodying these ideas, which may help to explain why the profession is dying. My humor can't compete with the Tea Party's reality.

Follow me, my friends, down the rabbit hole.

OBAMA WAS ACTUALLY BORN IN AMERICA TO SECRET BLACK COMMUNIST FATHER

Level Three Obama Truthers know the birth certificate theory was concocted by our Communist usurper as a red herring to make Americans look foolish. (Well played!) Obama's goat herding Kenyan father? A cover story for the real dad: Communist Party activist Frank Marshall Davis.

If you haven't heard of Davis before, that's okay, you weren't supposed to. He was a poet, autobiographical sex novelist, and teacher at Abraham Lincoln School, a Communist-run training camp in

Chicago. Subversive commie agents wanted one of their own in charge and what better way than to father one, raise him in secret as a Marxist, and present the "real" father as a foreigner? All that was needed was a pliable white woman to plant the seed into. Stanley Ann Dunham was more than eager.

Others point to Malcolm X as the clear father. (She got around.) He and Dunham are said to have both been in the same state at the time Obama was conceived and, of course, it's hard to imagine a black man being in the same state as a white woman and not impregnating her.

The case for Davis being the father remains strong. Looking at photographs of the two men clearly indicate parentage. The similarities between the two are jarring, including that both have two eyes, hair, and a single mouth located on the lower front region of the head. You can still tell even though Obama had plastic surgery on his nose to throw the scent off the trail.

OBAMA CAUSED EVERY DISASTER AND TRAGEDY THAT TOOK PLACE DURING HIS TERM—AND BEFORE!

Obama is a small, petty, incompetent man who cannot speak without the aid of the teleprompter and had Bill Ayers ghostwrite his book. On the other hand, he's pulled off a few modest capers in his time, like causing the BP oil spill, murdering Andrew Breitbart, faking Osama bin Laden's death, and causing Hurricane Sandy with a weather weapon that is also used to cause earthquakes and tsunamis the world over.*

The president also triggered the Aurora, Colorado, shooting (and all other mass shootings) in order to confiscate the guns of fun-loving Americans. Those false-flag operations with brainwashed government agents who are activated like Manchurian Candidates didn't quite do the trick, so he planned the Newtown, Connecticut, shooting, an untoppable spectacle of mass murder sure to soften up the public for gun confiscation schemes.

Obama has been the cause of every major event that has happened during his reign. "Ah, what about the recession?" you ask. It did begin before he was elected president—*I'll give you that much*—but the plot was hatched when Obama was a ruthless lawyer in a mortgage discrimination case against Citibank in 1995 that forced the honest bank to ease lending standards for poor, untrustworthy minorities who later gleefully defaulted on their house payments. Right before Obama takes office—BAM—recession, the likes of which we haven't seen in ages.

OBAMA IS THE ANTICHRIST

From a chain email forwarded to me by the girlfriend of a relative I never talk to: "The Anti-Christ will be a man, in his 40s, of MUSLIM descent, who will deceive the nations with persuasive language, and have a MASSIVE Christ-like appeal." Compelling.

OBAMA IS ALSO A GAY MURDERER

Larry Sinclair happened to meet Obama at the Chicago bar "Alibis" in 1999 and asked the State Senator to procure him some cocaine, as one does. Obama called his connect and they drove to pick up the white in Sinclair's limo. (Obama bought a modest amount of crack for himself.) Then they got high and had sex in the limo, as one does, with Sinclair giving O head without reciprocation. "Receiving blow jobs but not giving them would be consistent with Obama's narcissistic personality," wrote the keen observer, kreitzer, on the message boards for right-wing group Free Republic, where Sinclair posted his tale. Sinclair, upset that Obama was not mentioning these events during his quest for the presidency, wrote the book *Barack Obama & Larry Sinclair: Cocaine, Sex, Lies & Murder?*

---

* The High Frequency Active Auroral Research Program is real and does stuff with communications or something.

Obama, known to frequent bathhouses and carry on gay dalliances all over Chicago, was a member of Trinity United Church's "Down Low Club." This was a club where black dudes had sex with other black dudes and kept it on the Down Low. Some members didn't seem to be keeping up with their end of the bargain so Obama had to murder them before the election. Larry Bland was shot execution-style on November 17, 2007. A few days later the church's gay choir director was murdered in his home. A third member, Nate Spencer, was murdered with a triple combo of "septicemia, pneumonia, and HIV," presumably injected straight into his veins by Obama.

With his homo urges still needing regular attention, Obama tapped trusted fried Reggie Love—great name—as his "personal assistant," charging Reggie with carrying his coat, answering the phone, and performing frequent blowjobs. Kal Penn, of *Harold and Kumar,* was later hired by the White House to suck off Obama as needed.

"In a way, it's almost racist not to see Obama's gayness," kreitzer wrote. "We do have a tendency to assume all black males are high testosterone potential rapists."

Obama's slow shift towards being a non-asshole on gay rights has nothing to do with a personal evolution or political calculation—he simply wants to be able to marry a dude. "Obama will come out of the closet completely by 2013," Sinclair predicted. Who does Obama want to marry? Well, David Axelrod shaved his mustache at the beginning of Obama's second term after wearing it for nearly 40 years straight. Nothing, my friends, is a coincidence.

Obama is indeed calculating. If you were to have coke-fueled gay limo sex to later deny, what better mark than a self-professed drug-trafficker with a 27-year-long criminal record, including multiple convictions for forgery and fraud, and a 16-year prison stint under his belt? People would think he was telling tales out of school! Especially if the felon failed a lie detector test, the administrators of which were paid off by the Obama cabal.

OBAMA SENT A 75,000 WORD E-MAIL TO EVERY AMERICAN

"Having admittedly 'reached the end of [his] rope,' President Barack Obama sent a rambling 75,000-word email to the entire nation," reported the Onion News Network in 2010. "The email, which was titled 'A couple things,' addressed countless topics in a dense, stream-of-consciousness rant that often went on for hundreds of words without any punctuation or paragraph breaks."

Christ, what an asshole. Besides everyone in the nation receiving this dickish tirade, Fox News was the only media outlet with brass balls big enough to post a link to the Onion's blockbuster investigation. The rest of the bought-and-paid-for liberal media tried to act as if the president's psychotic fit were the mere musings of a humor writer in New York City working for a satirical news site.

"OK. Long, rambling tirade typed at 4 am. Judgment impaired as he didn't think twice before sending it. Didn't think of the consequences. Diagnosis: Bipolar Disorder," wrote trusted psychologist Jane Rogers in the Fox News comments section. "And we already know he has Narcissistic Personality Disorder. Omama [*sic*] is mentally unstable and should be removed from office at once."

"What you are seeing folks is the human unraveling and development of a self-delusional, irrational madman becoming unhinged. Can anyone say Hitler?" Mmttomb3 said in a post lacking in fundamental self-awareness.

"I must not be on his email list, I didn't get it," someone finally admitted.

Now, I don't quite remember reading this email either, nor does anyone I've ever met in my life (not that, come to think of it, I have ever asked anyone about it) but some people are pretty sure they read it.

"A friend of mine got the email because she was an Obama supporter," Bettybonnie posted. "She forwarded it to me. It was pitiful. My friend thinks he is losing it. I told her I knew this a long time ago."

OBAMA ONCE ATE DOG

True story.

OBAMA IS A CIA AGENT TRAINED ON MARS

Two time-traveling chrononauts, William Stillings and Andrew Basiago (a telepath), confess they encountered a young Barack Obama, then going by the name "Barry Soetoro," at the U.S. facilities on Mars in the early '80s during their participation in the CIA's Mars visitation program. That was the program, you may remember, where the Central Intelligence Agency teleported teenagers to the surface of Mars in order to establish U.S. territorial claims and acclimate Martians to a human presence via the quantum technology of the "jump room" located at 999 N. Sepulveda Boulevard in El Segundo, California. (It's all coming back to you, yes?)

The White House, sensing danger, officially denied the president's visit to Mars, but from 1981 to 1983 the man known to you as "Barack Obama" made at least two visits to the planet as evidenced by *the people who saw him there*. Stillings and Basiago have both stated Obama was in a Mars training

course run by Major Ed Dames. "Now we're here!" the future president said to Basiago upon encountering him outside the teleporter on Mars.

Dames, a psychic who ran the three-week training course preparing the teens for the jump room, told Obama, "Simply put, your task is to be seen and not eaten." Easier said than done. At the time, 97,000 pioneers had already made their way to Mars with only 7,000 or so living to tell the tale. (Or in this case, never mentioning it at all besides these two guys.) Interesting then that one of them would go on to became president, no? What are the odds.

Shhh. That's a rhetorical question. No one is that lucky.

OBAMA IS A MOTHERFUCKING SHAPE-SHIFTING LIZARD ALIEN

So everything above is true, with the small addition that Obama is a shape-shifting lizard alien from the lower level of the astral dimension, part of a race called the Anunnaki, who run the media, founded every global institution, control all governments, invented every religion, and who have trapped us

in a virtual reality matrix being broadcast from their moon base in order to feed off our fear, guilt, and aggression—their fuel. (Coincidentally the fuel for my soul as well.) Their favorite snack, however, is Earth's "monoatomic gold," which allows trans-dimensional travel, shape-shifting, and generally makes you an impressively smart lizard alien.

Peel back the layers of the conspiracy onion and at the center lies David Icke, a British football ("soccer") player who, after meeting with a psychic healer, went on to announce he was the "Son of the Godhead" and proceeded to pump out more than a dozen books detailing our mental enslavement. While it may seem like casting the first African American president as an inter-dimensional reptile enslaver has a racial edge to it, all sorts of white people are really lizards too! The really-are-lizards list includes George W. Bush, Queen Elizabeth II, various Sumerian kings, and Boxcar Willie.

OBAMA WAS VIDEOTAPED SUBMERGING A CRUCIFIX INTO THE POO SOUP OF HIS WHITE MISTRESS IN 1987

Well, that's not an actual conspiracy theory, rather something I pulled out of my ass. Buuuuuut since it's now in print, and someone will no doubt read the bold text without reading this explanatory text, breathlessly post about it on Facebook, sparking an irritating chain email that will live on for years and years and years, causing sane people extraordinary amounts of grief and frustration during holiday visits to their conspiracy-addled sort-of-racist in-laws, then, yeah, shit, I guess it is an actual conspiracy theory now. No need to thank me!

"Dear Mr. Bors, I believe liberals should be rounded up en masse and processed through concentration camps and the gas chambers. That's how I feel about it. America would be truly free if every leftist viewpoint were summarily exterminated. Thank you!" – James

AGENDA 21

THE INSIDIOUS U.N. PLOT TO **ENSLAVE MANKIND**

AND/OR

A NON-BINDING DOCUMENT ON SUSTAINABLE GROWTH FROM 1992

THAT ONE.

20 YEARS AGO THE U.N. CREATED AN OUTLINE FOR URBAN PLANNING AND MAKING CONSPIRACY THEORISTS SOUND BONKERS.

"AGENDA 21." THAT'S NICE AND SCARY-SOUNDING.

SECRET U.N. VOLCANO LAIR.

THIS IS NOT TO BE CONFUSED WITH **FOREVER 21**, THE EVIL PLOT TO STEAL YOUR MONEY VIA YOUR TEENAGE DAUGHTER.

BUT **MOM** I LIKE **NEED** THOSE PANTS **OMG!!!**

AS THIS PICTURE OF AL GORE TAKEN MID-YAWN AND AN OMINOUS MAP SHOW, **SOMETHING IS UP.**

IT STARTS SLOW, WITH BIKE LANES AND NIT-PICKY LAWS. THEN — **BAM** — YOU'RE A PRISONER HARVESTING TOFU IN MEGA-CITY 1.

MEET THE CARTOONIST!

This comic was drawn by Steven Q-640, the robot butler of George Soros.

GREETINGS, MEAT BAGS!

Steven is the cartoonist for Mega-City 1 and the 2053 Pulitzer Prize winner in cartooning. (If all goes according to plan.)

A popular conspiracy theory, paranoia over Agenda 21 culminated in Glenn Beck's 2012 thriller *Agenda 21*, which finds America under the control of the U.N. and now known simply as "the Republic." In this New World Order, "there is no president. No Congress. No Supreme Court. No freedom."

"Make way you communist sympathizer, we are on the MARCH from SEA TO SHINING SEA! So quit your illegal alien sympathizing and shut the FUCK UP. Our revolution will be victorious, and we will reclaim the lands which are rightfully ours. Step down pussy" – Armed and Dangerous.

88   LIFE BEGINS AT INCORPORATION

CROUCHING TEA PARTY, HIDDEN MUSLIM

U.S. OUT OF LADY PARTS

"I'm a huge supporter of women." – Rush Limbaugh

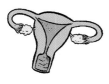 A massive war is underway in this country. At the demand of mean white men, it has been waged to varying degrees longer than any other war we've engaged in. Like the war in Afghanistan or the War on Drugs, this conflict is a pointless fiasco. Yet until common sense prevails, there will be a war on lady parts. Vaginas. Uteruses. Yonis, if you want to be annoying about it.

The men really burned up about the U.S. War on Lady Parts don't seem to understand how vaginas work. But they have a serious problem with them. There's ample evidence. And their many tiny victories are making things tough for good ladyfolk across the nation—and the men who don't actually want to control strangers' vaginas.

Politicians, especially those who profess to be deficit hawks, always evoke the American family's household budget when imploring us to gut some social program they hate. Now that they've cut taxes for decades, launched bank-busting wars, and destroyed the economy (all with the loving assistance of many Democrats), they are going after the true source of our fiscal woes: Planned Parenthood.

Depending on your point of view, Planned Parenthood is either a super-helpful spot for healthcare or a Fetal Genocide Machine. Me, I go there sometimes to make sure I don't have any diseases from all the pre-marital sex I'm having and think Fetal Genocide Machine may be the name of a metal band.

A majority of Americans have remained consistently in support of abortion rights since *Roe v. Wade* was decided in 1975. Despite this, conservatives have been steadily throwing up hurdles at the state

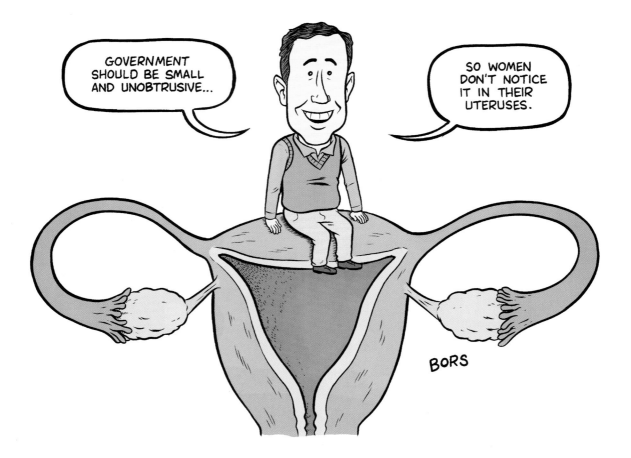

level ever since, to the point where abortion is effectively unavailable in large portions of the country. 2011 saw 92 abortion restrictions enacted—a new annual record.

In Texas, state law now requires doctors to be condescending douchebags toward women seeking abortions. Texas is one of eight states that passed laws mandating that women undergo vaginal ultrasounds—literally the definition of rape, but with a machine instead of a dick—before they can have an abortion. But that's not the height of the arms race in this war. A bill proposed in Tennessee sought to assist citizens in better locating abortion providers in order to murder them. I realize that sounds hyperbolic, but I can think of no other reason—even a bullshit one given for cover—for why the state would require publishing in newspapers the addresses of doctors. Printing this private information will very seriously threaten these doctors' lives.

Naturally, this proposed law was called the Life Defense Act.

While most voters will tell you they are primarily concerned with things like jobs, the economy, debt, and taxes, failed Republican presidential candidate Rick Santorum is holding it down for Americans who lament the nation's lack of Old Testament laws. What good is a job, anyway, if queers can marry? Santorum wants to ban gay marriage even in states that have already legalized it, re-institute "Don't Ask,

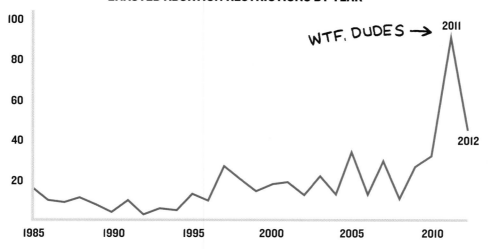

ENACTED ABORTION RESTRICTIONS BY YEAR

WTF. DUDES → 2011

2012

Source: The Guttmacher Institute

Don't Tell," and ban all women, including children who are raped by relatives, from getting abortions, even if giving birth will kill them. As if that weren't enough, he frequently wears sweater vests.

Santorum is the type of right-wing Christian who believes abortion is a holocaust, but who I bet would break every traffic law on the books rushing his unwed teenage daughter to Planned Parenthood upon her admitting that she was impregnated by a classmate. To these men, women are still treated as property.

Here's Iowa Representative Steve King in 2012 talking about why he's not real into outlawing dog fighting:

> What I've said is that we need to respect humans more than we do animals. Whenever we start elevating animals up to, to above that of humans, we've crossed a moral line. For example, if there's a sexual predator out there who has impregnated a young girl, say a 13-year-old girl—and it happens in America more times than you and I like to think—that sexual predator can pick that girl off the playground at the middle school and haul her across the state line and force her to get an abortion to eradicate the evidence of his crime, and bring her back and drop her off at the swing set, and that's not against the law in the United States of America.

That's a rather interesting defense of laws that protect doggies and an even more interesting notion of what exactly one can do with a 13-year-old girl without facing any legal repercussions whatsoever.

King, being a lawmaker, may actually be in a position to improve this situation, what with his ability to make law. I'm fairly cynical about the system, but I think even this Congress could muster 51 votes for the Raping Children Is Now Illegal Act. Obviously, King is spewing intellectually dishonest pabulum. His real issue is that abortion isn't illegal even in the case of a raped girl so he won't support any laws protecting low-ly animals, at least not until the fetus enjoys the same rights as his corporate donors.*

Look, I don't want to make it sound like it's only white males who make these terminally dumb statements about vaginas and the law. In 2009, anti-abortion activist Lila Rose told a Values Voter Summit: "If I could insist, as long as they are legal in our nation, abortions would be performed in the public square. Until we were so sick and tired of seeing them that we would do away with the injustice altogether." It would have a payoff, as the increased appreciation for life would result in "angels singing." To be fair, she admitted this "might sound a little strange."

Something else that sounded strange: When late right-wing agitator Andrew Breitbart confronted Occupy Wall Street protesters in February of 2012, he yelled "Stop raping people!" A video of the interaction went viral. As Breitbart was gently ushered away by security, he continued the bellow "Stop raping people! Stop raping people! Stop raping people!" and a thought occurred to me. Well, two. The first was that Andrew Breitbart was a drug-addled rage-aholic who was going to blow a ventricle if he wasn't careful. The second was that, yeah, stop raping people, people. That's actually a good idea.

North Carolina Defunds Planned Parenthood, "Great News" Says Cervical Cancer

A blob of malignant neoplasm seemed encouraged

While the Occupy movement was centered around economic and social justice, there were numerous reports of sexual assault in camps across the country. It was a dirty little problem that, like a lot of problems in the Occupy camps, reflected our larger society. It's estimated that 1 in 6 women in America will be raped in her lifetime. Most go unreported. Our military is the worst: A quarter of the women deployed to Iraq and Afghanistan have been raped. A third have been sexually assaulted.

There's been some confusion over what exactly rape is† and parsing out the finer details of what does or does not constitute this crime seems to be a popular male pastime.

The Avenging Uterus
@AvengingUterus

If your political party would perform better if we repealed women's suffrage, you're doing it wrong.

9:28 AM - 30 Aug 12

After Todd Akin presented his theory of "legitimate rape" and magic pregnancy prevention during the 2012 campaign, it was time to roll out the mostly-male pundits to sound off. Again, many of these dudes seemed to be unaware of how the female reproductive system even works, while others are just

---

* P.S. — King also thinks the 1961 birth announcement for Obama in the *Honolulu Advertiser* was sent in on an old timey telegram from Kenya, Baby Obama's homeland. It's amazing what you can get away with a telegraph. Too clever by half, Kenyans!

† It's when you rape someone.

intensely creepy. If you are so deeply interested in the minutiae of what does or does not constitute raping women, I'm a little worried about one leaving an unattended drink in your vicinity.

X-treme Libertarian Ron Paul was asked during the Republican primaries in 2011 if it was alright by him and his message of Personal Liberty if a woman would like to have an abortion after being raped. Paul's answer: Yes, sure, but only in the case of an "honest rape."

When you are bashing contraception, when you are whipped into a frothing rage over the Girl Scouts admitting a transgender child to their ranks, when you are inventing terms to minimize sex crimes, you have lost it. You might as well go all in and say vaginas have sharp teeth. Only olds can get riled up about gays and lady bits in numbers big enough to make it pay off politically—and thankfully they'll all be dead soon. Santorum, Akin, King, and other penis-havers might be utterly frightening,

KINDS OF RAPE
(According To Scumbags)

Legitimate Rape

Honest Rape

Date Rape

Asking For It Rape

Had It Coming Rape

No-Means-Yes Rape

"Rape" Rape

Rape "Rape"

and we aren't going to be rid of these dumb, sad fellows for a long time. But when I think about the assault on women's reproductive rights over the last few years, it's clear who has won the culture war and who is thrashing about wildly as they lay mortally wounded.

This is the right-wing's Battle of the Bulge. Things are looking great for them now, but Allied Forces are rallying. Someday, not quite soon enough, the Axis army will be abandoning their tanks in the snow and we will push them all the way back to Berlin, into their miserable bunkers of sexual shame to gnaw on cyanide tablets, followed quickly by parades. And sex. Lots and lots of sex.

Under the cavalcade of misogynist stupidity we faced in 2012, I came up with a recurring superhero, an actual anthropomorphic uterus, to physically combat this menace.

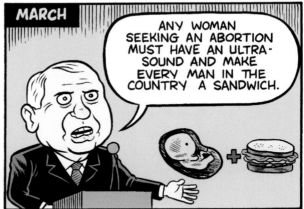

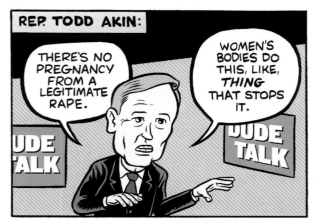

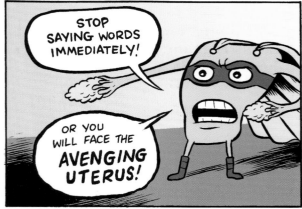

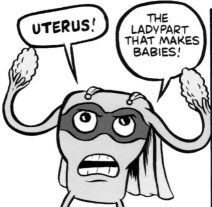

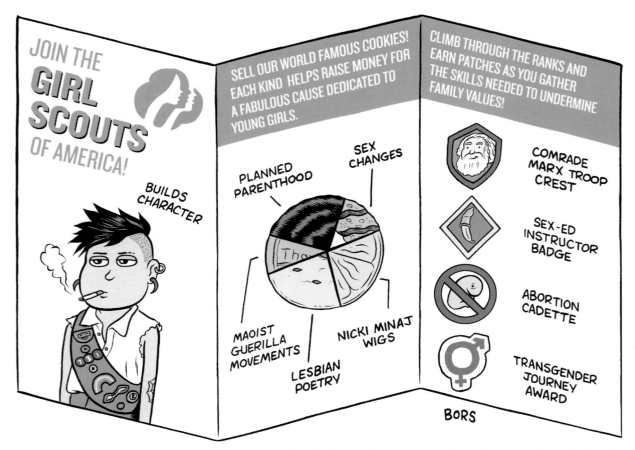

JOIN THE **GIRL SCOUTS** OF AMERICA!

BUILDS CHARACTER

SELL OUR WORLD FAMOUS COOKIES! EACH KIND HELPS RAISE MONEY FOR A FABULOUS CAUSE DEDICATED TO YOUNG GIRLS.

PLANNED PARENTHOOD

SEX CHANGES

MAOIST GUERILLA MOVEMENTS

LESBIAN POETRY

NICKI MINAJ WIGS

CLIMB THROUGH THE RANKS AND EARN PATCHES AS YOU GATHER THE SKILLS NEEDED TO UNDERMINE FAMILY VALUES!

COMRADE MARX TROOP CREST

SEX-ED INSTRUCTOR BADGE

ABORTION CADETTE

TRANSGENDER JOURNEY AWARD

BORS

The Girl Scouts are apparently a secretly subversive feminist front. After seeing people freak out over the admission of a transchild, I drew this updated pamphlet.

Dr. Ron Paul's Newsletter of Medicine

THIS WEEK'S INQUIRY:

Dear Dr. Paul,

When should a woman be allowed to seek an abortion?

-Piers Morgan

"If it's an **HONEST RAPE**, that individual should go immediately to the emergency room, I would give them a shot of estrogen."

Knowing if a woman was **HONESTLY RAPED** or simply wants an abortion can be difficult to determine. We recommend a rigorous [male administered] lie detector test to make sure the woman does not suffer from **HYSTERIA**.

IS INJECTING A SHOT OF ESTROGEN TAKING A HUMAN LIFE?

No, this is not an **HONEST ABORTION**. It differs from those procedures mainly in that I'm a man and have said so that's why.

Next Issue:
Back to Racism

CALL OF DOODIE

A MARINE WRITING IN **THE WALL STREET JOURNAL** OPPOSES WOMEN IN COMBAT BECAUSE... MEN TAKE POOPS.

It is humiliating enough to relieve yourself in front of your male comrades... it would be distracting and potentially traumatizing to be forced to be naked in front of the opposite sex

The arguments against women serving in combat roles are very intellectual.

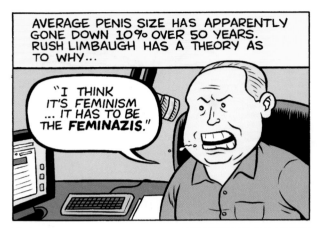
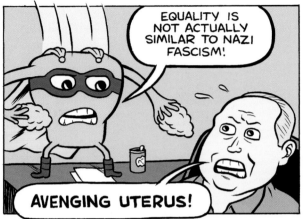

Sorry about putting that image in your head.

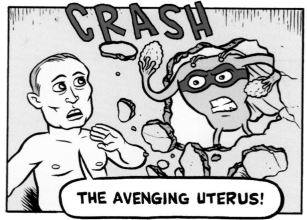

LIFE BEGINS AT INCORPORATION

AVENGING UTERUS ROGUES GALLERY

LIFE BEGINS AT INCORPORATION

MISOGYNO

REAL NAME: Vinny Brotelli

ORIGIN: As a lonely internet user, Menz_Rites89 trolled various blogs and Facebook groups making snarky remarks at anything written with a whiff of "feminazism." He fancied himself the "nice guy," resentful of ungracious ladies who owe him sex always putting him in the friendzone. It didn't help his situation that he wore a fedora.

One day, upon opening his estranged father's closet, a tower of *Maxim* back issues toppled onto poor Menz, crushing him. From that rubble emerged Misogyno: a hyper-masculine and buff freedom fighter, whose mental capacities shrank to make space for a freakishly expanded number of female beauty standards. An Incredible Hulk of the men's rights pity party, his battle cry can often be heard interrupting any and all intelligent conversation: "Misogyno Talk!"

ABILITIES: Intellectual fearlessness stemming from complete lack of self-awareness. Can consume large quantities of low-grade beer and/or Red Bull in a single outing. Power to bring to a dead stop every conversation, or use brute vocal strength to turn all discussion into a vortex-like audial phenomena revolving around the oppression of men and stupidity of feminism. Preternaturally loud. Able to post comments on the internet with machine-gun-like rapidity.

AFFILIATIONS:
Men's Rights Movement, Pickup Artist, MMA Fighting, AXE Body Spray

ENEMIES:
Women, Other Men, Himself

BASE OF OPERATIONS:
The Internets

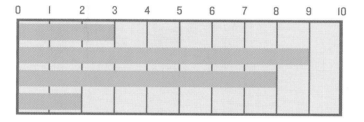

	0	1	2	3	4	5	6	7	8	9	10
INTELLIGENCE											
MUSK											
DOUCHEBAGGERY											
GRAMMAR											

DR. SLUT SHAMER

REAL NAME: Unknown

ORIGIN: Born to a single mother in Indianapolis, Slut Shamer showed early markings of intellectual promise in kindergarten. His mother worked three jobs to scrape together tuition to a prestigious private school. Struggling as a teen to relate to anyone his age, he instead lashed out at his mother, severing all emotional ties. As a teenager, he grew to resent romantic rejection, ultimately deciding it was he who rejected women as unworthy harlots.

Now under the belief that sexual activity is a sign of weakness, that short skirts provoke rape and sexual harassment, and that generally women get what they deserve, Dr. Slut Shamer is on a tireless quest to place blame for sexism on women. Operating out of a secret lair that looks suspiciously like a penis, Shamer develops robots and doomsday devices to unleash upon a sexually depraved society.

ABILITIES: Can pass harsh judgments with a single glance; believes he can read women's minds via evaluation of their clothing. Self-described as "very logical" with "genius-level intellect." Master of science degree in biology from the University of Ohio.

AFFILIATIONS:
None

ENEMIES:
Lindsay Lohan,
Dan Savage,
Anna Karenina

BASE OF OPERATIONS:
The Fortress of Morality

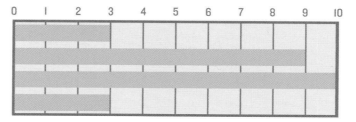

	0	1	2	3	4	5	6	7	8	9	10
JUDGMENT											
FAMILY VALUES											
PRUDISHNESS											
FASHION SENSE											

LIFE BEGINS AT INCORPORATION

THE MANDATORY TRANSVAGINAL ULTRASOUNDS

REAL NAME: None. It's a legion of vaginal wands.

ORIGIN: Developed in Dr. Slut Shamer's phallic lair, the robotic Ultrasounders are mechanical wands that spread fear and remorse in women when forcibly inserted transvaginally by the law. Dr. Shamer's conservative allies have aided in their plague-like infestation of several states, and mandated their use on women seeking an abortion in hopes of furthering their shame.

ABILITIES: Can produce an image of a fetus, thus provoking an occasional pang of sorrow, but otherwise useless.

AFFILIATIONS:
Dr. Slut Shamer,
Conservative State
Legislatures,
Right to Life groups

ENEMIES:
Autonomy,
The Sex-Positive
Dildos

BASE OF OPERATIONS:
Constantly expanding, but currently includes vaginas in Alabama, Arkansas, Idaho, North Carolina, Texas, and Virginia.

| 0 | 1 | 2 | 3 | 4 | 5 | 6 | 7 | 8 | 9 | 10 |

BATTERY LIFE

LIFE BEGINS AT INCORPORATION

75% OF WHAT A MAN MAKES MAN

REAL NAME: Harold Q. Carnoby, III

ORIGIN: Literally born with a silver spoon in his mouth, Harold Q. Carnoby III was the scion of steel baron Harold Q. Carnoby II's billion-dollar Carnoby Steel, LLC. Raised by a small army of nannies, maids, housekeepers, and tutors, 75 was proud to earn a legacy admission to Yale. He graduated after ten accomplished years and immediately lifted himself up by his bootstraps as appointee to a Caronby Steel executive position. Now Deputy Assistant Managing Partner at Carnoby Steel, the clean-cut son of privilege operates in the shadows as 75% of What a Man Makes Man, keeping wages low, denying promotions, and cultivating gender disparity in the workplace to reflect his deeply held belief that women truly don't work as hard as he did to get where he is today.

ABILITIES: Excels in promotion-blocking and nepotism. Building a corporate cone of silence policy, he can suppress a woman's paycheck for decades without her knowledge. With his well-exercised arm of privilege, he exerts downward pressure on all wages.

AFFILIATIONS:
Capitalism, GOP,
Howard Roark

ENEMIES:
Lilly Ledbetter,
The Supreme Court,
Human Resources

BASE OF OPERATIONS:
Your office, right now

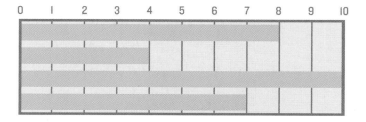

	0	1	2	3	4	5	6	7	8	9	10
INTELLIGENCE											
STOCK PORTFOLIO											
INCOME											
PRIVILEGE											

LIFE BEGINS AT INCORPORATION

FETUS FACE

REAL NAME: Stan Kroger

ORIGIN: Abandoned in a dumpster at birth, at least according to the fantastical "About Me!" page of his prolific blog, Kroger developed a passionate opposition to abortion and a "deep desire to protect God's little angels." He aims to create as many children as possible in his own life.

Fetus Face's first arrest was at the age of five after chaining himself to an abortion clinic's door in order to shut it down. His arrests became so common that police officers nicknamed him Fetus Face due to his unusual resemblance to a 20-week fetus. He embraced the name, festooning himself in graphic fetus imagery. Now 35, Fetus Face can be found bellowing insults every morning at 6:00 a.m. sharp outside the local women's health clinic (except Sundays, when he breaks for coffee and prayer). He regularly publishes poorly thought out diatribes on his blog amid lists of doctors' addresses, in case anyone wants to "pay them a visit."

ABILITIES: Ability to sustain protest without sleep for up to 48 hours. Owns a bullhorn. Higher than average babymaking ability due to aversion to contraception. Is "praying for you."

AFFILIATIONS:
The Pro-Life
Movement, Rick
Santorum,
Bob's Sign Store

ENEMIES:
Roe, Dr. George Tiller,
Plan B, Planned
Parenthood

BASE OF OPERATIONS:
The sidewalk

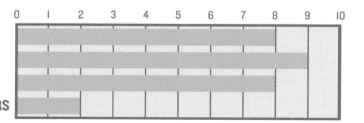

	0	1	2	3	4	5	6	7	8	9	10
RIGHTEOUSNESS											
HARASSMENT											
CHILDREN											
RESTRAINING ORDERS											

DEAR GUN NUTS

"America was born on guns and whiskey." – Alex Jones

After the first time I shot a gun, I couldn't hear anything for two days. This is because it was a .44 magnum and because I was eight and not wearing any ear protection. It's a huge gun—the kind Dirty Harry used—and my dad had to help me hold it as I pulled the trigger. The next day, he had to explain to my third grade teacher why the only thing I could hear was a loud ringing.

There are right ways and wrong ways to go about your gun-having. (And your son-having.) My dad did do a good job of teaching me about gun safety once I was able to hear him speak words again. He even went and bought ear protection. Growing up around guns made me feel comfortable with them. So, gun owners, I'm not against you.

For a while, the 60 percent of Americans who don't own personal firearms had a hard time figuring out how to communicate in the jargon of gun people. But over the course of the last few dozen national conversations after mass shootings, we've all become armchair experts in arsenals. Was the killer using hollow points or full metal jacket rounds? Big difference. Is there a collapsible stock on that Bushmaster AR-15? Oh, he used Colt pistols instead of Glocks? Weird.

After every mass shooting—which is essentially all the time these days—gun rights advocates drag out the "more guns = more safer" argument. And yet: we're still not safe! Despite having almost one gun for every man, woman, and child in the nation, peak safety has yet to be reached.

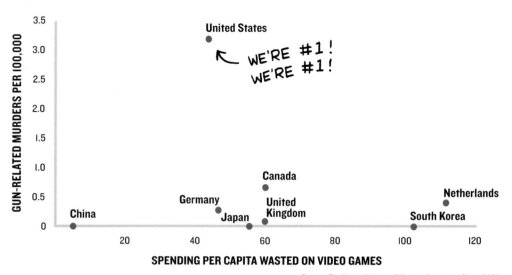

GUN-RELATED MURDERS AND VIDEO GAMES

Source: The United Nations Office on Drugs and Crime 2007

Now. You're allowed to oppose gun control on grounds that restricting the ability to purchase a gun violates your second amendment rights and will leave you up shit creek without a Smith & Wesson when it comes time to overthrow a tyrannical government. And I agree that many proposed gun control laws won't do anything, especially patchwork ones put forward in response to mass shootings. Most murders are committed with handguns and banning those is not even on the table. Some dudes wrote the Second Amendment on piece of paper a while ago and we all have to live with the result of that. But you know what we can do in lieu of new laws? Change our culture so fewer people die every year. Gun people, we need to talk about your behavior a bit.

First of all, can you stop saying video games cause violence? They don't. Countries where people play way more video games than we do have lower rates of gun deaths. The thing about violent video games is they don't feature characters going around killing people with video games. They use guns. Or Hadoukens or Babalities or stuff.

Which brings me to my second point: Guns kill people. They are not made for pressing sandwiches or sopping up grape juice spills in the kitchen. Guns are specifically designed to propel bullets through a person's body at a velocity sufficient to kill them. Saying "guns don't kill people, people kill people" is not an argument for more people having guns. You just said, sir, that people kill people. Guns are inanimate objects full of deadly potential. How do we help them realize their destiny to be peaceful, non-lethal objects and keep them away from *people*?

Lastly: You're carrying around an assault rifle in public because...? I know you are not out on a killing spree, just a nice stroll, but it's...sort of hard to tell? Insisting on carrying your gun in public is like asserting your free speech rights by screaming at everyone you see. No one is saying that isn't "legal," but we're not looking at you like you're Rosa Parks. More like a total douche. The fact that

you are intentionally drawing police attention smacks of crazy privilege. The Black Panthers used to carry arms in public—usually didn't end well for them. I'm a white guy who is not homeless and thus have a low risk of incurring police brutality, and even I know better than to involve police unless it's utterly necessary.

Firearm technology is one of those things that really could have stayed frozen in time two hundred years ago and we'd all be doing fine right now, really. There would still have been plenty of opportunity to get our war on and defend our homes with single shot muskets you had to arduously reload by hand. The playing field would be even for criminals, do-gooders, and armies alike.

Instead, now guns are a multi-billion dollar industry and the only way to keep making money is to foster a climate of fear that drives people to purchase all sorts of tactical, military-style weapons no one could possibly need. One of the most powerful lobbying groups in America is the National Rifle Association and their name is apt: The NRA is an association representing rifles (and other guns), not you. They're playing you. The paranoia they're pushing is designed to get you to put more of your money in their pockets. You probably don't need to have so many weapons for self-defense. You can

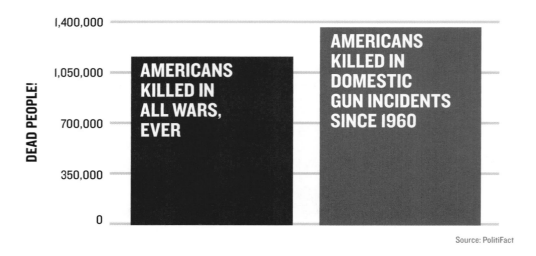

DEAD PEOPLE!

1,400,000

1,050,000

700,000

350,000

0

AMERICANS KILLED IN ALL WARS, EVER

AMERICANS KILLED IN DOMESTIC GUN INCIDENTS SINCE 1960

Source: PolitiFact

only really use one at a time. And guns are sturdy products. They aren't falling apart all over the place. Get rid of some of yours and go buy yourself a nice pair of boots. You'll look great!

If you take the positions of the NRA and add them up, you can see how the world would look if the gun lobby got everything it wants: Every American would have easy access to assault weapons, gun dealers would not be required to check the criminal record and mental health history of someone before selling them a gun, the capacity of gun magazines could be near-infinite, and it would be illegal for a city to stop people from carrying guns in public. This would be a country where you could literally buy an AR-15 at Walmart, immediately put on full tactical gear worn by SWAT teams, and stroll into a school for your parent-teacher conference with another fully armed adult. Practical!

You think I'm anti-gun. I'm not. I think of guns like I do cars. Go ahead and own one. Waste your money on something fancy!

But the scenarios you are preparing for aren't going to happen. You aren't going to save the day by shooting a terrorist in the grocery store. We need fewer guns so fewer people shoot their feet off, kill their girlfriends, kill themselves, and go on shooting sprees.

You can have guns for hunting. You can have them to ward off Mexican drug lords or whoever is going to storm into your house. Keep them there, in a locked safe. And if we by chance ever need a well-regulated militia for a revolution or zombie apocalypse, by god, we're going to be really happy you were born with a micro-penis.

OVER 100 KILLED IN PAKISTAN BOMBINGS

WOULDN'T HAVE HAPPENED IF EVERYONE HAD A BOMB.

In states that allow open carry, Starbucks has not put up signs prohibiting guns inside its stores as many businesses do. Gun-rights advocates took note and launched a supportive 'buycott.'

It's rare that an editorial cartoon ever breaks news, but I was the first person to report anything on this insurance program, which was then picked up by ThinkProgress and other outlets. Hear that? It's the sound of a man tooting his own horn.

LIFE BEGINS AT INCORPORATION

WELCOME TO
THE TERROR DRONE

"You have 20 seconds to comply." – ED-209

War is a great thing to watch from a safe distance.

During the Civil War, families would gather on a hillside to picnic with their children and watch cannonballs rip men's limbs off. It was a nice way to spend the day, particularly if the weather was pleasant and your side was winning. CNN brought back the grassy hillside in 1991 with its Gulf War coverage: tracers and explosions lighting up the night sky on your TV screen. You didn't exactly get the full effect—you couldn't smell the blood in the air—but war hadn't been this exhilarating for viewers for at least the last half dozen ones America had started.

I follow our nation's drone strikes on Instagram these days. Every attack is updated so you never miss a one. I can get an alert for my phone so it will interrupt me during sex. I don't activate it, but I like having the option.

Science fiction until recently, unmanned aerial vehicles—drones—are the new, neat way of killing. Touted as a safe way to cut down on unnecessary death, drone strikes are executed with "extraordinary care and thoughtfulness," according to the Obama administration, to do away with the people in other countries whom he says are terrorists—including Americans. You can tell drones are only for killing bad guys and not the innocent guy who happens to live across the street from the bad guy because the two most popular drone models have namesakes famous for reducing civilian casualties: Predator and Reaper. A new, smaller model put into action in 2011 launches out of a little portable

device soldiers carry. This lets soldiers dive-bomb it into nearby people by remote control. It's called the Switchblade Drone, after the knife that is illegal because it's only for stabbing people in their gut so they bleed to death.

Right now, surveillance drones the size of insects exist and I'm sure some bright ~~war criminal~~ entrepreneurial engineer is hard at work devising ways to turn them into lethal mosquito-bots.

The next step is truly self-aware drones that call all the shots and won't give operators PTSD as they dwell on who they've killed. (Truly, a first world problem.) The machines will eventually turn on us, slaughtering humans in what the history books will cast in a very positive and forgiving light, because it will be robot history written by robots. Oh, we'll get everything that's coming to us. I'm more concerned about what it's going to be like before Skynet eradicates us.

The rules governments devise for killing people are constantly evolving. Not that they have a very good track record at actually adhering to their own rules in the first place. Chemical warfare was once on the cutting-edge of science, but has since been deemed bananas. Unlike mustard gas, drones are okay to use because they are "conventional weapons," which means they are the weapons we are currently using to kill people today. Assassination is also a thing of the past, not acceptable to engage

in under international law. Thankfully, Obama is operating a program of "targeted killings" not at all like assassination, and with a set of rules and safeguards held in complete secrecy for your benefit.

One rule is that America won't kill you unless you are "affiliated" with a terrorist organization. What's affiliated mean? Well, if you're dead, it means they decided you were affiliated! Not only that, but you were determined to be an "imminent" threat. This is where I'll pause to make a George Orwell reference.

Can the U.S. attack you anywhere? Yes, according to the rules, the entire planet is fair game because we are engaged in the War on Terror. Currently, that we know of, the CIA is knocking people off via robot missiles in Afghanistan, Pakistan, Yemen, Somalia, and Libya. What's off limits? The moon. Go there.

Drones raise all sorts of interesting questions about the way to most ethically murder people. The White House insists our deployment of deadly robots is "legal, ethical, and wise." Is it any of these? To get to the heart of this quandary, first I want you to kill someone with a sword. Not a loved one or anyone who is contributing to the world in a significant and worthwhile way, but some bad guy no one will call you out on. Make a determination and run them through with a sword. Go on. I'll wait.

...

Okay, kind of messy, isn't it? I'm imagining a struggle and a hot mess of blood everywhere. You got a work out (good) but your eyes met with your victim's and you may have seen them as a human being (bad). You may have had a few doubts about killing someone because a cartoonist told you to do so in a book.

Now try killing them from your home computer with a joystick that controls a drone. You can probably listen to the Yeah Yeah Yeahs and keep a few browsers tabs open while you do this. Choose a place where CNN hasn't set up shop and people are too poor to own camera phones. We can't have people posting that depressing shit on Facebook all day.

The Bush and Obama administrations' rules for the War on Terror do not prescribe any precise method of killing. We could "put dynamite in their behinds and drop them from 35,000 feet" as talk show host Michael Savage once suggested. Hell, we could drop them from the edge of space and slap a Red Bull label on 'em if we wanted! But drones are what we mostly use.

Since Obama took office, he's racked up a lot of skymiles with these global Robocops. He's especially fond of using them in Yemen, where a few hundred people have been killed in strikes since he took office. Thing is, the people left alive are often unhappy about these attacks and motivated to join

the fight against Great Satan. Al Qaeda membership in the Arabian Peninsula has more than doubled since 2009. Maybe they need…more drone strikes?

If Americans don't care about Yemenis (and let's admit it: they don't) they should at least care about their own ass. On September 30, 2011, Obama authorized the execution of American citizen Anwar al-Awlaki for being affiliated with Al Qaeda. In a strike a few weeks later, al-Awlaki's 16-year-old son, Abdulrahman, was also killed. He too was born in the U.S.A.

Asked how he defended the attack, former White House Press Secretary Robert Gibbs said al-Awlaki should have "had a better father." And he should have. We all should have had better fathers. But Americans have the right to fair trial and to have charges brought against them. Instead, the president maintains he has the right to kill people he deems guilty. This right is not found in the constitution anywhere, but it does say so right in *Judge Dredd*, section 17:32. That's good enough for most people.

Drones are proliferating faster than we can make up made up rules for them. I can buy one right now and fly it around my neighborhood filming people. Police departments are starting to use them for surveillance purposes and I'm sure they won't use them excessively and disproportionately against the poor and minorities, the way they've used every tool ever plopped into their palm—batons, mace,

guns, and tasers. Other countries are perking their ears to the thought of armed drones. Something tells me Americans would object to Cuba coming after sworn enemies of their regime by firing hellfire missises into a Miami neighborhood.

Our robot death planes aren't ensuring that we only kill the Bad Guys. They allow us to not have as much skin in the fight, so less is revealed to us about the nature of killing. Improved technology does not equal acting more moral. The wheel was pretty great, unless you were being tied to one and tortured to death on orders from men with righteous and good intention.

But it's not the robots I'm worried about. It's us.

If we can save the life of even one child, Obama said, we should take that step. He was talking about guns.

Our government can't afford to deliver anything to your house on Saturday unless it's a missile.

LIFE BEGINS AT INCORPORATION

THE ONE PERCENT DOCTRINE

"Get a job after you take a bath." – Newt Gingrich

 Do the rich have enough money yet? Just curious. Many of America's ultra-rich individuals keep whining about how rough they have it. Indeed, people call them mean names on the internet and a few politicians still remain who are not devoted to rigging the entire economic system for their benefit. And then people like me come along and make fun of them in cartoons. It's a hard knock life.

As the gaping chasm between the rich and the rest of us opens wider every day, the put-upon megawealthy demand more in the form of less: fewer regulations, lower taxes, more cuts to government programs. They've been successfully chipping away at the New Deal for decades and apparently won't be satisfied until with we are all reduced to medieval serfdom.

The top one percent of Americans now have 35 percent of all nation's wealth. The bottom 80 percent are left with 11 percent to divide up amongst ourselves.

Imagine being on a life raft with one hundred people and one guy in the corner is hoarding 35 percent of all the supplies. He'd be kind of an asshole, yeah? If some people threw him to the sharks, you might be inclined to cheer.

When the rich were finally endangered by their own money-vacuuming system with the 2008 financial crash, politicians responded to it like a four-alarm fire. The $700 billion bailout of Wall Street's speculative trickery—passed under President George W. Bush and supported by then-candidate Barack Obama—was the largest transfer of wealth in human history. Further economic mea-

sures included a stimulus package with too many tax cuts instead of meaningful jobs programs, and the extension of the Bush-era tax cuts that mostly put money into the pockets of the wealthiest Americans.

So you'd think, given those extraordinary actions, the top one percent would simply pause for a minute and say, "You know what? We're doing alright here, let's lean back and rest on our giant beds made of money."

But no, they want the government to fluff their pillows as well. To hear the rich complain about their lot in life is to take a trip into a Bizarro World of bellyaching where the lower classes are the ones getting all the breaks. If you believe conservative talk radio, the winners of our society are the people who "mooch" off government checks: people who are permanently disabled, unskilled immigrants, single women who have multiple children. It is apparently easy to be poor. But I've yet to see an investment banker give up his gig so he can collect food stamps and live the easy life.

The bailout and Great Recession killed off the myth that America is a meritocracy. Real unemployment hit 17 percent. There was no public works program like there was during the Great Depression because that would be "socialism." And socialism is bad. Instead, most of the money from the bailout

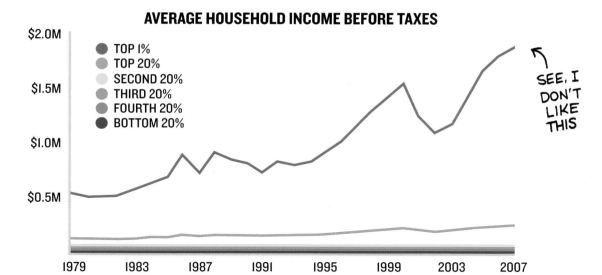

AVERAGE HOUSEHOLD INCOME BEFORE TAXES

- TOP 1%
- TOP 20%
- SECOND 20%
- THIRD 20%
- FOURTH 20%
- BOTTOM 20%

$2.0M
$1.5M
$1.0M
$0.5M

1979 1983 1987 1991 1995 1999 2003 2007

SEE, I DON'T LIKE THIS

Source: Congressional Budget Office

and stimulus went to the rich. Class mobility was now something only experienced by lottery winners. The years dragged on.

Then came Occupy. Glorious, messy Occupy.

Suddenly, in the fall of 2011, thousands of people were camped inconveniently in public spaces, talking about class, raging against income inequality, and using funny hand signals—and they weren't leaving. Suddenly there was an actual left. Finally the nation was talking about the issues that crush its citizens into debt dust. The usual avenues for change had proven ineffective. Perhaps there was promise in smashing the state after all.

"I like the idea of revolution," cartoonist Shannon Wheeler told me when it all started. "On the other hand, I'd really like to catch the last season of *Breaking Bad*."

Scrapping the system entirely is a lot work. Most people have jobs they have to show up at.

The Occupy movement was criticized for being disorganized and without clear legislative goals. What did these protesters want? Why didn't they go vote Democrat or go to work in the nonprofit world? As a political cartoonist, I felt these were my people: free of party, existing on principle, believing in a completely unrealistic idea of what can be accomplished. Coalescing around a 4.25 percent increase on marginal tax rates would have sapped all of the spirit from the movement.

WE ARE THE 98%

1% OF OUR POPULATION IS IN PRISON

Occupy's legacy can't be measured by legislative accomplishments, but rather how it planted class-consciousness into the minds of average Americans. Occupy was a beautiful little thing for that short time before it fell apart. Which was also right about the time it was torn apart by police with military efficiency.

In the winter of 2011, I went down to Occupy Portland's encampment in the center of the city every day during what turned out to be the camp's last month of existence. Political activists abounded, but Juggalos and street kids made up an ever-increasing percentage of camp residents. After a while, who else but them had time to camp in a park night and day? While I was there one afternoon, one kid overdosed right in front of me and had to be carried out on a stretcher. This wasn't exactly great PR for the birth of a new movement.

But in the end, it was the clubs and tear gas that ended the Occupations, not the moochers and drug addicts. In November 2011, city and campus police forces across the country staged a not-at-all-coordinated (wink wink) effort to storm Occupy's camps, using various levels of force to destroy most of the physical headquarters.

If the nation's wealthiest people set up shop in a park to fight for a tax cut on capital gains, the police would form a protective barrier around them to ensure their safety while the mayors delivered donuts and shook hands.

Two sketches from the final day of the Occupy camp in Portland, a city that is also the corporate headquarters of Nike.

And since when did our cops start dressing like shock troops from a science fiction movie? In Portland and across the country, police were geared up in face shields and black body armor. All sorts of nice toys were purchased for them with Homeland Security money. They even have weird sound ray cannons now in case terrorists—or hippies—gather for a protest and then blast out of the area.

Occupy itself fizzled, but that movement's energy still exists out there. The problems at the root of the movement certainly haven't been fixed. The rich are still winning. Still whining. I'm wondering if we can get them to at least stop subjecting us to their griping as sort of a consolation prize for them having all the money.

Wealthy Americans literally have better lives than anyone who has ever existed in the history of forever. Human history's most decadent emperors would be floored by the luxuries enjoyed by your average rich kid. Julius Caesar never got to drive a Hummer. We normals also benefit from eons of the human achievement (and, uh, slavery) our society is built on, and we enjoy the distinct privilege of being born in the richest country that has ever existed in the history of human civilization.

But the problem is that when one of us loses our job, our health, or our house, no one is there to bail us out. No amount of hard work will ever boost most Americans into a realm of economic security. It is nice that we have magic phones now, though.

At this point, politicians are entirely unresponsive to almost all actions that don't involve lobbyists putting cash directly into their hands. Changing this absurd system takes more than holding your nose and voting for the lesser of two evils on Election Day. Sometimes it takes holding it in a cloud of tear gas next to the Juggalos.

LIFE BEGINS AT INCORPORATION

IF JANITORS WERE LIKE CEOs

IN AMERICA, YOU CAN PLUNGE THE ECONOMY INTO AN ABYSS OF DEATH AND GET A RAISE.

DUMP TEN TRILLION BARRELS OF OIL IN THE OCEAN AND NOT EVEN BE LATE TO YOUR YACHT RACE.

LAUNCH INSANE WARS, BURN THE CONSTITUTION, TORTURE MUSLIMS AND RETIRE COMFORTABLY TO PEN YOUR MEMOIRS.

TRAVEL BACK IN TIME, KILL GEORGE WASHINGTON, ENSLAVE AMERICA WHILE DRESSED AS DOCTOR DOOM AND BLARE JUSTIN BIEBER SONGS 24 HOURS A DAY WITHOUT ANY OPPOSITION.

HA   HA HA

BUT DON'T LET A REPORTER FROM **ROLLING STONE** QUOTE YOU TALKING SMACK ON OBAMA...

BIG POOPY HEAD.

YOU WILL BE HELD **ACCOUNTABLE!**

NO POTTY MOUTHS RUNNING MY QUAGMIRE.

BORS

please vote.

LIFE BEGINS AT INCORPORATION

LIFE BEGINS AT INCORPORATION

JUDGMENT HOUSE

"I'm sorry you don't believe in miracles." – Lance Armstrong

 At my first and only Catholic confession, the priest asked through the screen of a small wooden booth what I wanted to confess. I was eight years old and nothing jumped out to me. The priest tried to help me along, suggesting that maybe there was some area of my life where I was falling short of god's ideal. Had I not honored my father and mother as he commanded? Had I stolen anything recently? The only real confession that I could come up with was that I should share the Nintendo more with my little brother. The priest said that, yes, I should share the Nintendo more. We prayed together about Nintendo sharing, he and I, to the creator of the universe.

I remember being completely baffled as to why this conversation between a child and adult needed to take place, or what kind of god would want it to occur. It dawned on me that adults maybe didn't have this whole god thing figured out.

I attended a weekly Sunday School class and by the time I reached sixth grade, I was an atheist, though I didn't know there was a name for it, nor did I tell anyone about my doubt. One week a nun was waiting at the front of the classroom to inform us our teacher died in car wreck. Although our teacher had claimed Satan once tried to break into our world through an Ouija board, I had thought of her as one of the most down-to-earth people there. She was more interested in helping people than observing the bizarre moral codes and rituals that occupy the time of the Catholic clergy.

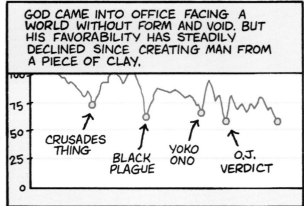

The nun told us students that we needed to pray for our teacher and I pretended to do as I was told. I remember wondering whether god would not let her into heaven if we didn't pray hard enough. Wasn't this more for our sake than hers? More troubling to me: If her eternal fate was determined on the backs of desperate pleas from children, is this a god we should be speaking with regularly or figuring out how to eradicate?

Sixth grade Sunday School wasn't the appropriate time to ask those questions, but then, there's never really a "right time" to challenge religious people. It's always rude to question religion. I'm not talking about arguing over the age of rocks or the science of evolution. That stuff is settled. I'm talking Deep Brain-Busters here. Like why trust god's version of events in the first place? He could just be a fancy alien wanting attention and wowing us with technology so advanced we view it as heavenly. If you time-traveled back to medieval times with an iPad you could tell those vitamin-deficient morons anything and they'd worship you.

I stopped going to Sunday School and church entirely around the eighth grade and embraced my atheism. As a heathen, I'm not very interested in proving god doesn't exist. I'm more interested in figuring out why people who believe in him believe in him. What I mean is, if a supreme deity truly

does lord over our every thought, why does that automatically warrant obedience? You created the cosmos and all life on earth. Thanks, I guess, but maybe let us do our own thing.

God seems needy. And really big on getting you to fall in line through fear.

In 2006 I went to a haunted house for Jesus in Norton, Ohio. The Jesus haunted house was not a traditional haunted house—they called it "Judgment House"—it was something run by the Grace Brethren Church during the Halloween season to draw in those who are curious and gravitate toward free things. Like me.

The idea was that you walk through a set of rooms and watch terrible teenage actors play out dramatic scenes that show them straying from the path of Jesus and down the dark road to the unimaginable sin of drinking at a party. (Sample dialogue: "I like drinking because I don't have to THINK about anything!") Lead character Mike goes on to die in a drunk driving accident, taking another person down with him.

Now dead, Mike takes a stroll with Jesus through a room full of filing cabinets stuffed with all of his sins. (Heaven hasn't switched to electronic records yet.) Jesus asks, "Should Mike get into heaven?"

In the last room, at the Pearly Gates, Mike begged for forgiveness. But it was too late! He hadn't accepted Jesus Christ into his heart and thus was ushered into hell. Cue flashing red lights, agonizing screams, and high schoolers banging chains against the wall. Killing people (and yourself) in a drunk driving accident sure is a bad move, but spending more than one hundred quadrillion years in hell for it? Seems excessive.*

Why does everyone who believes in god seem to approve of his weird-ass moral system? The conflicting beliefs of the Christian god overlap almost perfectly with his flock. For example, people who believe that dudes who do other dudes in the butt will burn in hell argue that god agrees with them. Meanwhile, religious people who aren't homophobic, and who think even Buddhists and atheists go to heaven as long they aren't Hitler, also believe that god agrees with them. Everyone who's religious says they're following god's lead. Now, I don't want to blow your mind with another one of my theories, but I think maybe they're looking to god to justify their own personal views of morality.

* In a stunning shock ending, it turns out it was all a dream! Mike passed out drunk at his friend's house and dreamt the whole dying and going to hell thing...or did that sly old dog Jesus plant that dream in his mind? Either way, Mike was reborn a Christian. Phew!

I'm ready to meet a devout believer who rejects god completely as a dictatorial asshole. I'd love to encounter a fundamentalist Christian who has come to believe—through logical reason and the clear supporting evidence—that the earth is 6,000 years old, hell is a literal place, and god sends almost the entire human race to burn there forever. And I want this believer to think that this god is a horrible deity.

Maybe gays are okay, he thinks. Maybe being tortured forever for a few infractions is a little...psycho? But no matter what, he can't shake the fact that, yup, that specific god exists and there's nothing he can do about it.

For the obvious reasons, I've never found this kind of believer. But there are a few signs that people are beginning to question god's job performance.

About 20 percent of the country is irreligious these days. And young people are giving it up in record numbers. God is getting the ol' phase-out, like someone you're dating but just aren't that into anymore. He really needs to work on himself for a while before anyone should consider him "relationship material."

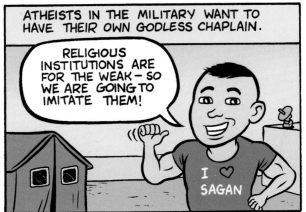

A 2011 poll by Public Policy Polling found that god enjoys an approval rating of 52 percent with Americans. While higher than any politician, that's rather unimpressive for an omniscient, all-powerful being. It was found that five percent of Americans disapprove of god's handling of the creation of the universe. There is discontent brewing out there.

The people lingering outside of the Ohio Judgment House were not part of that doubting group. Some of my fellow haunted house–goers had been moved to tears by the fictional events and talked loudly about their decisions to recommit to Jesus. A teenager deeply affected by our tour told me, "The hell scene—all of it was real. It showed me how much more there is to life!"

That's the response the house is supposed to provoke. The pastor at Grace Brethren told me he started the whole thing in order to portray "real life."

"We've got people in the ministry that come to Christ through Judgment House," he said. "This gets us energized. It's our most effective outreach program."

I asked if Judgment House was an example of using fear to get people to obey god.

"People live in guilt and shame and they don't have to," he replied.

Precisely.

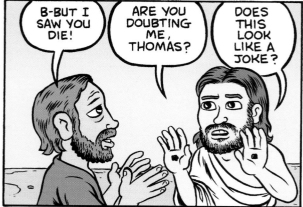

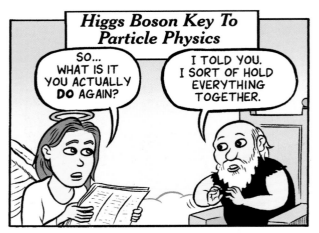

At some point I drew god as an overweight balding beach bum. It worked, so I kept him around.

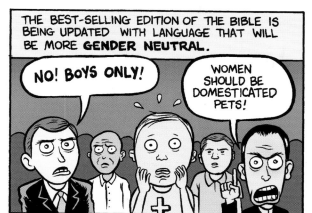

THE BEST-SELLING EDITION OF THE BIBLE IS BEING UPDATED WITH LANGUAGE THAT WILL BE MORE **GENDER NEUTRAL.**

NO! BOYS ONLY!

WOMEN SHOULD BE DOMESTICATED PETS!

IT IS ALL ACCORDING TO **GOD'S WILL**, AS HE TOOK A COURSE IN WOMEN'S STUDIES AT YALE THIS LAST SEMESTER.

HAD I READ DWORKIN OR STEINEM EARLIER, I TOTALLY WOULD HAVE SPARED LOT'S WIFE.

THIS IS WHAT A FEMINIST LOOKS LIKE

DESPITE LINGERING QUESTIONS, GOD'S GENDER WILL REMAIN **MALE** IN THE UPDATED TEXT.

I'M NOT **REALLY** A DUDE, BUT I HAVE TO APPEAR LIKE ONE FOR PR PURPOSES.

IF THE CREATOR LET **THAT** SECRET OUT OF THE BAG, HIS WHOLE FLOCK WOULD TURN **ATHEIST!**

I AIN'T WORSHIPPIN' NO **HERMAPHRODITE!**

KEEP THIS **SMUT** AWAY FROM CHILDREN!

BORS

LIFE BEGINS AT INCORPORATION

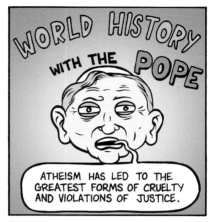

LIFE BEGINS AT INCORPORATION

DRIVING BIN LADEN

"It's only because of their stupidity that they're able
to be so sure of themselves." – Franz Kafka, The Trial

If you drove a known terrorist around, does that make you a war criminal?

Could be. The federal government loves stretching terms like "aiding and abetting" and "providing material support" to the outer bounds of absurdity. Given their penchant for overreach, I might be an eligible drone strike target thanks to a cartoon of mine that made it all the way down to Guantanamo Bay, providing aid and comfort and humor to Osama bin Laden's driver, Salim Hamdan, during his military show trial in 2008.

Typically, when I include someone in a political cartoon, I fantasize about them reading through the panels and immediately crumpling into a ball, overwhelmed by my devastating wit. But though I had been drawing cartoons about our most infamous and outrageous overseas prison camp for years, I never thought my little cartoons run in free alternative weekly papers would make their way inside its wall and into the hands of one of its victims.

Afghan resistance forces picked up Salim Ahmed Hamdan in southern Afghanistan in 2001. In his car, the soldiers found two SA-7 surface-to-air missiles, $1,900 in cash, and five photos of his baby daughter. He was turned over to U.S. forces—sold for $5,000, Hamdan says—and transferred to Guantanamo Bay the following year.

Hamdan admitted to being Osama bin Laden's personal driver—hey, he needed the money—and was cooperative with the U.S. the whole way—hey, he wanted out of prison. The guy caught driving a dusty Toyota hatchback around the desert to make ends meet would be tried in the first American

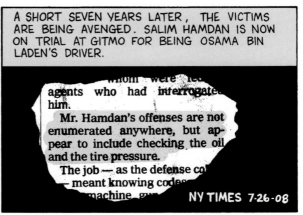

military commission for an alleged war criminal since World War II. We'd come a long way from Nazi doctors. This was frying a small fish.

His case went all the way to the Supreme Court in *Hamdan v. Rumsfeld*, which ruled that the country's brand new military tribunal process violated the Geneva Conventions (a no-no). So the U.S. continued to hold him, passed the Military Commissions Act in 2006 to deal with it, and charged him again. One of his military lawyers, Brian Mizer, told me Hamdan was kept in isolation the majority of these years, and by the time he faced trial for "providing material support" to Al Qaeda, he was only hanging on by a thread.

"Everything our laws and Constitution say cannot happen to a person happened to him," Mizer told me. "And that was evidenced by the discussion he had with the judge at one of our last pretrial sessions."

"He held up a white piece of paper," Mizer says, "and showed it to the judge. He said, I tell you this paper is white. You tell me no, it is black. I say fine, it is black. Then you say, no it is white. That is American law."

It's easy to forget how crazy we got after 9/11. Many of us have blocked the trauma of the Bush years, others have always been happily oblivious to the things being done in America's name. Really though, most people were blindly supportive of our new legal hellscape. After our invasions, we swept

up thousands of Muslims and kept them in secret prisons, in CIA black sites in 54 countries, and on ships so they'd be outside the reach of law. We shipped them to countries to have them tortured, then shipped them somewhere else.

In faraway prisons like Abu Ghraib, detainees who hadn't been charged with any crimes were smothered in shit, collared with dog leashes, stacked naked in human pyramids, and had electrodes attached to their genitals. Some of this systemic torture was written off as the frat boy antics of bored "bad apples" in the military. The rest was fully justified with creative legal theories.

When John Yoo, President Bush's Assistant U.S. Attorney General, was asked in 2005 if the president had the power, legally speaking, to crush the testicles of someone's child in front of their eyes in order to get them to cooperate, he replied, "I think it depends on why the president thinks he needs to do that."

Guantanamo's detainee camp was established quickly in January 2002. Overnight—poof—it went up and we started housing people from all over the world without charges, including teenagers. At its peak in 2005, Guantanamo held nearly 800 people. We even held Uighur dissidents for the nice guys running China because they asked us to. Detainees were tortured. Some were murdered. Some committed suicide. Some remained for years and died of natural causes.

Waterboarding, once considered torture, was now an "enhanced interrogation technique." Other enhancements to our techniques included sexual humiliation, pissing on Qurans, sleep and sensory deprivation, and years of isolation that eroded a person's ability to think.

By the time he confronted the judge in 2008, Hamdan's lawyer Mizer says his client was despondent from years of isolation in a foreign prison he thought he would die in. When I drew a cartoon about the charade that was his trial, the magic of the internet brought the comic to Hamdan's lawyers. Mizer had it translated and I dropped a signed print in the mail, addressing it to the naval base in Cuba.

I'm often accused of helping terrorists out with my work, but only in the form of emails where people say things like, "I certainly hope somebody beheads you soon!"

Mizer has a much more hands-on job of helping alleged terrorists: He defends them in court.

"All military personnel take an oath to defend the Constitution. And that is an abstract principal for most of us," he says. "But it was very real for those of us defending the detainees as we struggled to get the government to recognize our most basic values."

"Does a man have a right to due process before he can be deprived of his life and liberty? Must he be brought to trial quickly, and face his accusers in open court? Sadly, despite our founders enshrining these rights in our founding documents, the answer to all of these questions is no."

While campaigning, Obama promised to shutter the camp. But he quickly back-burnered that promise once elected, then quietly removed it from the stove altogether. In 2009, he embraced the idea of indefinite detention without a trial. The detainees were stuck in a made-up legal process that seemed to have no end. One idea—to transfer Gitmo detainees to U.S. soil—proved a non-starter with Congress. No lawmaker wanted to host them in their state. Senators who tout their tough-on-crime credentials and steer money to private "supermax" prisons that round up their constituents were suddenly acting like they lived near Arkham Asylum, where maniacal villains break out on a weekly basis to plot a new attack on Gotham.

In March 2013, Sulaiman Abu Ghaith, Osama bin Laden's son-in-law and Al Qaeda spokesman, was brought to New York City and indicted in federal court on conspiracy charges after being arrested in Turkey. Senate Republicans howled, claiming that trying him in a real court somehow endangers the country.

The remaining Guantanamo detainees sit and wait.

"If some of those men have committed crimes under domestic or military law, then they should be tried by a federal district court or court-martial," says Mizer. "The judicial system functioning at Guantanamo Bay is illegal."

In October of 2012, Hamdan's conviction was overturned by a three-judge panel on a D.C. circuit court that included a Bush appointee. Proving material support for terrorism wasn't a war crime when Hamdan was picked up in 2001. They made it so, then tried him retroactively.

Can't do that, the judges ruled. Can't make shit up. Driving bin Laden isn't a war crime.

"The entire judicial system was forged after the fact, from the crimes to the rules and procedures," Mizer says. "That is virtually unprecedented in human history."

Some people—me—don't get why the so-called War on Terror requires a new set of rules. Or rather, why the rules need to be smeared in shit, stacked in a human pyramid, and called fine and dandy. Mizer says legit terrorists should be held like prisoners of war in World War II: housed in military-style barracks, then charged.

The system at Guantanamo is a sham. The last two presidents say you can hold these men forever without charges. And Americans have short attention spans. The public at large seems to barely remember the outrages we subjected thousands of people to, or that 167 people are still rotting in Cuba.

Hamdan wouldn't mind never hearing from the U.S. government again. The government dropped him off in Yemen in 2009 the same way he was taken out of Afghanistan years earlier: with a black bag over his head and cuffs around his wrists. He lives in anonymity now and avoids speaking to the media about his time in the American justice system. He's just trying to support his family these days doing what he does best.

If you ever hail a taxi in Yemen, he could be your driver.

OBABA ANNOUNCED HE WILL HOLD GITMO DETAINEES INDEFINITELY FOR CRIMES THEY **MAY** COMMIT IN THE FUTURE.

THEY HATE US SO MUCH FOR IMPRISONING THEM THAT WE CAN'T RELEASE THEM FROM PRISON.

AT THAT RATE, WHY RELEASE ANYONE FROM PRISON?

30 DAYS FOR DRUNK DRIVING AND **LIFE** FOR PROBABLY DOING IT AGAIN.

WE NEED A **DEPT. OF PRE-CRIME** TO CRACKDOWN ON ALL FUTURE FELONS.

IN A MOMENT I'LL SHOOT YOU TO DEATH FOR JAYWALKING—SO I'M ARRESTING US BOTH **NOW!**

AND SINCE PRE-CRIME ITSELF IS ILLEGAL, OBAMA CAN START THERE.

KEEP ME AWAY FROM THE CONSTITUTION!

BORS

Iran arrested three American hikers who had crossed into their country and tried them in a court of law before agreeing to release them. If only our detainees were so lucky.

SOCIAL MEDIA IS A SCAM

"How are you feeling, Matt?" – Facebook

The internet is a whole thing I don't even want to talk about. Ugh. Mostly I don't want to talk about it because of how people on the internet will talk about it—and that's what I really want to talk about.

Specifically, I want to talk about social media.

While they apparently seemed like a good idea to all of us only a few short years ago, sites like Facebook, Twitter, and their ilk have taken over our lives and the way we interact with each other, all for the benefit of a very small amount of mostly horrible people.

The people benefitting from these sites have perverted the English language by turning everything they touch into marketing buzz-speak. Words like engagement, conversation, like, friend, experience, share, and connect used to mean something deep, sweet, and genuine. Now, they have lost all meaning as marketers transform our online experience (see, I used one!) into a giant, self-promotional circle jerk.

Social media is a scam.

Now, hey. I'm not down on everything about these sites. The book you are reading? Funded by 725 generous people through Kickstarter. I've made friends—real ones!—through social media. I've gotten paying gigs through social media. I've gotten laid because of social media. So some scam, right?

I present these qualifiers because criticism of internet culture is typically met with a pile-on from the hive mind. I'm not necessarily against being in touch with every single human being you have ever attended school with, dated, or worked alongside. But to quote a meme, we're doing it wrong.

The internet was once a freewheeling place filled with promise, but giant corporations have assimilated online media institutions and social networking sites just as they once swallowed up independent television and print media. YouTube was gobbled up by Google, Instagram swallowed by Facebook. Huffington Post merged with AOL. These sites employ relatively few people, but we're all helping their executives shovel money into their Scrooge McDuck vaults.

While there's a tendency to act as if social media exists for the sole purpose of helping the world grow happily interconnected, in truth they exist to glean our personal data and consumer habits in order to sell them to the highest bidder.

In Jaron Lanier's book *You Are Not a Gadget*, he lays out his case against the current incarnation of the internet, specifically social media and its insidious business model. Lanier on how the scam is a scam:

> [O]ne must remember that the customers of social networks are not the members of those networks. The real customer is the advertiser of the future, but this creature has yet to appear in any significant way. The whole artifice, the whole idea of fake friendship, is just bait laid by the cloud lords to lure hypothetical advertisers—you might call them messianic advertisers—who could someday show up.

As a pioneer of early virtual reality technology (think *Lawnmower Man*) Lanier is not exactly a Luddite. And he's right about the overhyped nature of these sites—both financially and culturally. Facebook's public stock offering famously flopped. How, exactly, does one "monetize" our daily status updates? I've been on Facebook for years and can't recall a single ad I've seen on there. Facebook actually makes extremely little cash per user, but CEO Mark Zuckerberg is a billionaire because so many of us are pathetically on the site so often.

Thankfully for us, this is an incredibly dumb model. I believe it will collapse as companies realize that people "liking" a Facebook Pringles page does not result in more Pringles sales. It just means people clicked a button, probably on accident. As these sites struggle to demonstrate profitability, they integrate—there's another word I hate—more advertising, making them a more obnoxious waste of time.

It's bad enough that we're filling Mark Zuckerberg's moneybags with our sad self-promotion and needy life updates. Unfortunately, social networking has the added drawback of making us all act like assholes toward one another. Comment sections are infamous pits of vitriol filled with every form of insult and discrimination imaginable. Yet most news outlets have them to encourage "debate" and "reader engagement"—by which they mean provide a platform for fighting in order to milk a few more cents from Google ads.

Anything that facilitates immediate contact between opining strangers devolves into bad things. Unfortunately, I have a great personal example of this.

On December 14, 2012, the morning of the school shooting in Newtown, Connecticut, I was watching the news unfold online and trying to wrap my mind around being a part of the human race. CNN named Ryan Lanza as the suspect suspiciously early. Within minutes, journalists at several outlets were not only reporting the name, but passing around a link to Ryan's Facebook account. And people I knew were suddenly telling me, "Dude, you're Facebook friends with a mass shooter."

His wall was set to private so I was one of the only people seeing Ryan post "Fuck you CNN it wasn't me" and "IT WASN'T ME I WAS AT WORK IT WASN'T ME" as television networks and

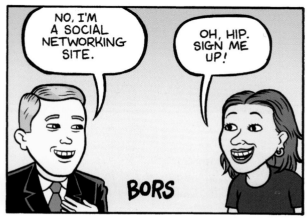

websites posted photos pulled from the account. I posted a screen shot to Twitter and Facebook to let everyone know that this Ryan Lanza, at least, was not dead at the scene of the crime.

That's when things got crazy for me.

The screen caps spread fast and I found myself inundated with messages, some from journalists seeking confirmation, but mostly from people saying angry and bizarre things to me or about Ryan. One demanded to know how I could be friends with such a monster. Could I help a random internet sleuth create a "psychological profile"? Did I see warning signs in Ryan? Why did I suspiciously post cartoons about mass shootings only days before? That was very tasteless. A text to my phone from an unknown number read "looks like this killer is a fan of yours." A Twitter user declared me a "snitch" for sharing Ryan's post. Someone accused me of having something to do with the killings, "which you take delight in," they wrote, adding that they hoped the FBI would hold me accountable.

Lanza, it turned out, was the brother of the killer, but I didn't know him. I assume he was like most of my Facebook friends in that he likes to follow my work. That's what my Facebook account is for: sharing my brand engagement for exposure. And, man, I'm starting to hate it.

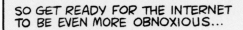

As someone who's used to getting their share of criticism and trolls, the "feedback" on this one was on a level that surprised me. Not two hours after accusing me of being involved in the killing of 20 children, one of my angry Facebook messengers was back: "I apologize for jumping the gun."

I know this is an extreme example, an unlikely coincidence during a rare news event. But it was only a few factors stronger than what happens every microsecond on the web, where any mention of, well, literally anything can set off a flame war. Online, we're not thinking straight.

There's some evidence that people are growing tired of the constant upkeep required to maintain their social media lives. It's just too damn tedious and draining to constantly "engage" like this. Social media purports to connect us but it often does the exact opposite. It encourages the worst in people while sucking away our most precious resource—time—to line the pockets of the cloud lords.

We all want out but we have to be on social media because everyone else is. It doesn't have to be like this. We can liberate ourselves from their scam and start over.

On the count of three, everyone unfriend each other.

What do you think? Leave a comment below and join the conversation!

SOCK IT TO ME

I once live-tweeted a meeting of sock entrepreneurs at my neighborhood coffee shop. This is the best use of Twitter I've come up with so far.

Matt Bors @MattBors   March 17, 2011 10:50 AM
People behind me in coffee shop having business meeting about socks. Terms I'm hearing: "hip branding," "fun," "funky!" and "Tweeting"

Matt Bors @MattBors   March 17, 2011 10:51 AM
Do not brand your socks as "funky," marketing people. They will not sell.

Matt Bors @MattBors   March 17, 2011 10:56 AM
I'm learning the ins and outs of sock company marketing here, folks. Let me know if you have questions and I'll ask these entrepreneurs.

Matt Bors @MattBors   March 17, 2011 11:02 AM
Father's Day is the biggest day in a sock company's life.

Matt Bors @MattBors   March 17, 2011 11:08 AM
Serious talk about how to get the socks on the Today Show and gain "viral momentum" for the socks.

Matt Bors @MattBors   March 17, 2011 11:11 AM
There is a woman, she is a "foodie and great blogger," and she can help get the word out about the socks.

Matt Bors @MattBors   March 17, 2011 11:12 AM
"what's our narrative?" How about: Socks go on feet.

Matt Bors @MattBors   March 17, 2011 11:13 AM
Another big time in the sock world: back to school shopping. Huge.

Matt Bors @MattBors   March 17, 2011 11:21 AM
"It's not just a company." No, really. It is. You sell socks.

Matt Bors @MattBors   March 17, 2011 11:23 AM
Some sock companies aren't honest. This one is. It's part of their mission. Also in the mission: socks covering feet.

Matt Bors @MattBors   March 17, 2011 11:25 AM
Biker goes by with knee socks. Instant speculation as to what brand they are.

Matt Bors @MattBors   March 17, 2011 11:29 AM
Just heard a sentence with all these words: local, opportunity, outreach, building, brand, and socks. I can't reconstruct it. I'm sorry.

Matt Bors @MattBors   March 17, 2011 11:34 AM
"what are socks to people?" They... are... socks?

Matt Bors @MattBors   March 17, 2011 11:35 AM
turned around. Sock entrepreneur not even wearing socks! Bro!

Matt Bors @MattBors   March 17, 2011 11:39 AM
These socks "really have potential." Other, quickly: "Oh yes. Oh yes. People respond well to them." (SOCKS!)

Matt Bors @MattBors   March 17, 2011 11:47 AM
Ooo. They are standing up! "It's been productive"

Matt Bors @MattBors   March 17, 2011 11:51 AM
Folks, this was an historic meeting. This company could be huge. I feel like the guy who live tweeted the Bin Laden raid.

PAY NO TRIBUTE

"You have the words of eternal life." – St. Peter

 Someday you will die.

It's impossible to predict when and where. But, if you happen to be a well-known figure, it will be easy to predict with startling precision what the world's editorial cartoonists will work up for your obituary cartoon.

You will no doubt be found at the Pearly Gates uttering a variation of your most famous phrase, drawn tastefully with the dates of your birth and death underneath, or gone entirely, represented by an item closely associated with you—a product, a logo, a cartoon character—inexplicably shedding a single tear.

The illustrated tribute to the dead celebrity remains alive and well, especially with artists who have to pick the kids up early from soccer practice.

In over 1,000 editorial cartoons, I have only noted the death of someone four times. I rarely venture into this territory, finding it almost completely unnecessary. For many cartoonists it has become an easy out for a work day. For me, there are simply so many other things I'd rather cartoon about than marking the death of some poor schlub.

It's not paying tribute to important figures that I object to—it's the sheer predictability of the tributes. The clichés are as certain as death and taxes, and almost as infuriating. And their relevancy and power has diminished along with shifting attitudes about humor and reverence.

We live in the age of instant reaction—and instant mockery. The celebrity death cycle now shifts from shock to fond remembrance to snark before the body gets cold. Illustrations still have the power to bottle any one of those sentiments for preservation, but a tribute that adds nothing to the conversation is as disposable as a tossed-off tweet.

Within thirty minutes of finding out about the death of Steve Jobs, I predicted he would be depicted arriving at the Pearly Gates of heaven telling Saint Peter "There's an app for that" as he flipped through his book of whatever that book is. That cartoon did materialize—and not just once, but in no fewer than twenty cartoons. Jobs was a Buddhist, but don't let that get in the way of a bad idea. There's something about marking the passing of an innovator with an interchangeable cliché that really speaks to the current vitality of the field.

The imposition of a literal heaven by editorial cartoonists (a generally godless bunch) upon anyone of any religion is often defended as a simple tradition: the way we tell jokes 'round here. Perhaps Pearly Gates cartoons are a bit like the traditions of human sacrifice and bloodletting—best left to historians who specialize in cataloging Things That Seemed to Make Sense at the Time.

The single teardrop is another trope that will puzzle future generations of tasteful humans. Meant to elicit a deep loss, the Apple logos crying for Steve Jobs only reminded me I need to get my MacBook to a Genius Bar before the crack in the screen gets any bigger. The most famous single tear ever teared was featured in the American anti-litter public service announcement, "The Crying Indian," where a Native American was shown with a single tear tracing down his face while he faced piles of litter. Litter made him sad. It quickly became one of the most widely parodied and ridiculed ads in American history. The somber teardrop rolling solo down a sullen face sort of did a switcheroo after that and became more an ironic thing used by hip youngsters. The year was 1971.

I often hear that tribute cartoons are some of the most popular cartoons out there, which I think is similar to the argument Michael Bay used while pitching his third movie based on toy robots.

Editorial cartoons should strive for more than popularity—they need to address the issues of the day, not just mark the passing of time with illustrations of news events. They must confront the public with the thing that isn't being said. They must prove they are still relevant. While the maudlin tributes and cheap jokes poured in on Steve Jobs, *The Onion* carried the torch for satire with the article "Apple User Acting Like His Dad Just Died." It could have been about my peers.

Cartoonists are supposed to hold a public figure's life up to the light and scrutinize them, not draw them heading towards the light while glorifying them. Yet not a single cartoon critical of Jobs emerged until I drew one over a week after his death. Maybe he is an unassailable genius after all. Chinese factory owners certainly appreciated him.

Editorial cartoons work best when they are dishing out biting humor. They can do somber, or powerful, or sad, but the situation has to be right and the execution perfect for it not to collapse under the weight of its own seriousness. The automatic churning out of tribute cartoons for even the most minor celebrities is born more of laziness than respect for the dead.

In a world with so many outrageous things to be made fun of, I am rarely compelled to stop and pay tribute in a cartoon. Not when I'm racing towards my next target for satire while eyeing the one after that. So many deserving topics. So little time.

Someday I will die. Spare me the tributes.

There is a lot I liked about Hitchens and he was kind enough to give me a blurb about my work. Nonetheless, his support of the Iraq War tarnished his legacy as a brave rhetorical pugilist. He never had a problem speaking ill of the dead so I'm sure he wouldn't mind.

ASSORTED CALAMITIES

 The following batch of comics contains my take on some major issues, some forgotten ones, and attacks on mortal enemies like Justice Scalia and Pope Benedict. Racism, environmental collapse, censorship, the abolition of privacy rights, and other cheery topics are all touched on, and—oh, just go read them and I'll stop talking because we're near the end of the book.

AMERICA'S ENERGY SACRIFICES

I BELIEVE IT WAS BEN FRANKLIN WHO SAID:

THOSE WHO SACRIFICE LIBERTY FOR SECURITY DESERVE A GOOD PAT-DOWN.

HE WOULD HAVE BEEN GREAT AT AIRPORT SECURITY, LIKE **NED BLIPPLE**, TSA'S EMPLOYEE OF THE MONTH.

EYE-BALLIN' YOUR JUNK

NED'S AN INNOVATOR, COMBINING THE SEARCH FOR UNDERGARMENT **TERROR** WITH SCREENING FOR **BREAST CANCER**.

CHECKING FOR LUMPS...

AND BRA BOMBS!

IF YOU WANT TO CATCH A FLIGHT IN TERMINAL C AT CHICAGO O'HARE, YOU HAVE TO GET TO SECOND BASE WITH NED.

DON'T WORRY, MA'AM. I'M A MASSAGE SCHOOL DROP OUT.

SAVING LIVES FROM AMERICA'S GREATEST FOES. THAT'S NED.

TWO BIRDS WITH ONE GROPE!

BORS

LIFE BEGINS AT INCORPORATION

A NEW EDITION OF **HUCKLEBERRY FINN** WILL REPLACE THE WORDS "NIGGER" AND "INJUN" WITH NICER ONES.

READ AND RELAX!

ALSO TWEAKED FOR LANGUAGE...

A SLIGHT REVISION

SHE'S 18!

NOW BLANK FOR PUBLIC DECENCY!

FULLY ABRIDGED

NEW UPLIFTING EDITION!

THEY GROW OLD TOGETHER AND DIE OF NATURAL CAUSES.

SPIEGELMAN'S **MAUS**: JEWS REDRAWN AS BALLS OF YARN. SAME GREAT PLOT.

"PLAYFUL" – **TIME**

BORS

Father Gary Thomas became certified to practice exorcisms after completing 40 hours of study at the Vatican.

LA TIMES 1-27-11

AND REMEMBER: "CASTING OUT SPIRITS" IS NOT A LEGALLY ACCEPTABLE DEFENSE FOR TOUCHING CHILDREN.

"I know that in today's immoral and upside down world view, the sacred is no longer respected. It MUST STOP! I'm sending the offensive cartoon to the Catholic League. I hope they will investigate this offense." – Carmela

One of my pet peeves is the instance that we are in some era of great incivility and that everything was rosy before cable news shout-fests came along.

When I traveled to Haiti to head up a comics journalism project for Cartoon Movement about recovery efforts from the 2010 earthquake, I saw a dysfunctional state where the government provided hardly any services. In other words, a Libertarian paradise. Yet you don't find too many people tripping over themselves to move there.

Opponents of the health care reform bill insisted that the fine levied for not buying an insurance plan was actually a tax. In a floor debate in the House during one of the many votes to repeal Obamacare, Rep. Jim McDermott of Washington used this cartoon to show how ridiculous the GOP argument was.

After Hurricane Sandy we realized there might actually be ramifications for pretending that global warming isn't happening.

KICKSTARTER ROLL CALL!

This book couldn't have been made without the backing of 725 people through Kickstarter. The following were especially generous in their support for this book.

NM GUINILING
BRIAN GILMAN
CHRISTOPHER EGGERTSON
MICHAEL DUNN
DAVID & AMANDA MITCHELL
SARA THAVES
NATASHA YAR-ROUTH
TRUFFER PATRICK
RON KRETSCH
NATHANIEL SHERDEN
DAVID BALLARDO
STEVEN CLOUD
GLENN FLEISHMAN
BECKY BORS

WARREN BERNARD
ANNIE KOYAMA
AARON ANDERSON
JAMES STENOISH
TOMER CHEN
AIMEE SMITH
JOHN BATES
JASON HARTWIG
LEIGH STOLLER
RENEE BROOKS
NICHOLAS MEYER
SUMIT KHANNA
PHIL & LORI BROOKS
JACK WHITE

LIFE BEGINS AT INCORPORATION

ACKNOWLEDGEMENTS

This book couldn't have been done without the support of my Kickstarter backers who straight up paid for the printing costs by pre-ordering the book and trusting me to create something worth their money.

Some good friends helped me put this together. The talented writer and reporter Sarah Mirk was my editor for the text and tightened my rambling rants into coherent, readable chapters. In some cases, jokes that I get to take credit for originated with her. We've collaborated on a number of projects at this point and I can't wait for the next.

Jessie Carver originally came on as the copyeditor and her involvement kept growing as my print deadline approached and I couldn't handle it all. She served as a project manager, working with the printer to work out specs and costs, compiled the index, and generally kept me on schedule with her Google Doc skills. I wouldn't have got this book done on time if she weren't more generous with hers. As a sign of my appreciation I even conceded to her desires in regards to the Oxford comma.

Kathleen Barnett managed to knock out the layout and design under the gun, make it look exceptional, and deal with all my nit-picking fussiness like it wasn't even a thing.

Masheka Wood created charts, the inside cover, and colored a number of the comics in here so I could focus on the writing. He's performed these feats on a number of projects with me now and is owed beers.

Glenn Greenwald, Jessica Valenti, Markos Moulitsas, and Christopher Hitchens graciously provided blurbs. If anyone ever cared what a cartoonist thought, I'd return the favor. Jack Ohman is part of my posse even though he moved to Sacramento. Jack, did we ever pick up those frames?

John Glynn at Universal Uclick, wrote me back a decade ago, long before anyone was reading my work. Now I'm syndicated through them and Reed Jackson has been fixing my typos for years. Thks, buddie! Ted Rall invited me to Afghanistan and brought me into my first syndicate deal. That would have been enough but then he became a close friend and supporter.

A number of people have helped me get to this point in my career, which as this book goes to press is now ten years old. There are too many to thank by name, but some whose support led straight to the creation of this book in some way are Tony Kuhar, David Halperin, Joshua Holland, Tom Tomorrow, Glenn Fleishman, Dylan Meconis, Dan Olson, Patrick Truffer, whiskey, Keith Knight, David Axe, Marci and Alex at The Herblock Foundation, The Daily Kos crew, whoever invented Kickstarter, my parents, and Stephanie for being patient.

INDEX

WWW.MATTBORS.COM